幾ノ如キ高性能特□速ノ機体ニアリテハ取扱及整備上ノ些細ナル不注意モ優秀ナル性能ヲ害ヒ本来ノ機能ヲ発揮シ得ザルハ勿論時ニ重大ナル事故ヲ惹起スル事アルベキヲ以テ之ガ取扱整備ニ関シテハ綿密細心ナル注意ヲ払ウ要アリ　零式艦上戦闘機ノ取扱上本書ト併セ参照スベキ図書ノ主ナルモノ下記ノ如シ　十二試艦上戦闘機実験（第一回報告　空技廠研究実験成績報告第二六九六号）

零戦
ZERO FIGHTER

Text by ROBERT C. MIKESH
Illustrations by RIKYU WATANABE

Jane's Publishing Company Limited
London · Sydney

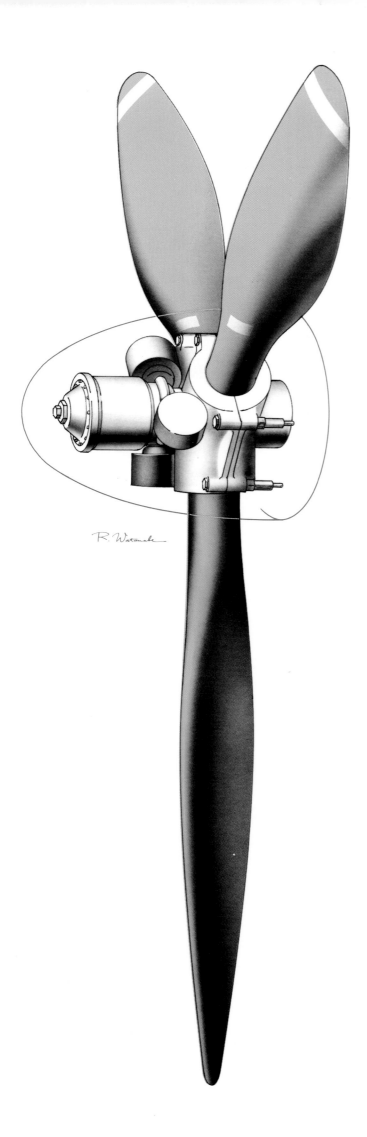

R. Watanabe

Acknowledgements

My sincerest thanks go to all who have helped in developing this story of the Zero fighter. Particular appreciation goes to Shorzoe Abe, David A. Anderton, Walter J. Boyne and René J. Francillon. The letters, books and personal contact with Jiro Horikoshi and Saburo Sakai have provided the foundation on which this history has been developed. To all, I give my deepest thanks.

Translation of Japanese text on end-papers:

Imperial Japanese Navy Aviation Headquarters, *Rei-shiki* Carrier-borne Fighter Plane Manual (1936).

Introduction

This publication has as its aim a statement of the standards of instruction necessary for a high maintenance of the Rei-shiki carrier-borne fighter craft, and to provide reference for its various personnel. The data assembled and included in this manual are obtained both from the design and planning data of this craft and also from the various records of experimentation. Since, however, each plane incorporates structural variations, it is essential that further specialized materials, relevant to each model, be consulted; and that the completed inspection-result sheets of actual-flight records should also be studied so that the characteristics of each model may be fully absorbed.

This is a craft of very high capabilities, especially as in regards speed. This being so, even the slightest error in servicing or handling this plane would not only detract from the superior qualities of its performance but could also lead to serious accidents. Therefore, the closest attention in both servicing and piloting must be observed.

This book was designed and produced by Wing & Anchor Press, a division of Zokeisha Publications, Ltd., 5-1-6, Roppongi, Minato-ku, Tokyo 106 & 123 East 54th Street, New York 10022.

© 1981 by Zokeisha Publications, Ltd.

First published in Great Britain by Jane's Publishing Company, Ltd., 238 City Road, London, ECIV 2PU.

Printed and bound in Japan.
First printing, February, 1981.

ISBN No. 0 7106 0037 2

First Blood

Twelve Mitsubishi Zero fighters of the 12th *Kokutai* turned away from the Chinese city of Chungking and headed back toward Hankow. Below, billowing columns of smoke mushroomed from the stricken city, the result of well-placed bombs dropped by an Imperial Japanese Navy force of 54 Mitsubishi G3M2 Type 96 Bombers (later to be code-named "Nell" by the Allies). The Zeros, flying on their first combat mission, had been detailed to escort the bombers to the target and back.

Lieutenant Tamotsu Yokoyama, a recent arrival from Omura Naval Air Base, led the fighter formation. Earlier in the flight he had given the signal to his pilots to arm their weapons, but much to their disappointment, not a single enemy fighter was sighted. This first mission of the new A6M2 fighter, on 19 August, 1940, was a bloodless one.

Previous escort missions had been flown by another Mitsubishi fighter, the A5M4 model (known later by the Allies as "Claude"), with open cockpits, fixed landing gear, and limited range. They had gone with the bombers as far as they could. More aggressive Chinese interceptions during the past six months had begun to hurt the Japanese; their losses were rising. The new Zero fighter arrived on the scene none too soon, for the vulnerable bombers needed protection all the way to the target and back, and the Zero had been designed to do just that.

Type 96 Carrier-borne Fighter (Mitsubishi A5M4) "Claude"

But where was the Chinese opposition that had been so plentiful on previous missions? The Zero pilots could hardly wait to engage the enemy, for they knew they had the superior machine. But the Chinese, noted for their intelligence-gathering ability, apparently could foresee the Zero's deadly capability, and knew when this first mission was taking place. There was no contest in the air that day.

The next day it was the same. Formation leader Lieutenant Saburo Shindo hoped he would have the chance to engage the enemy for the first time with the Zero. He and his wingmates returned to Hankow without firing a shot.

These Zeros, introduced to operations in the late summer of 1940, were part of a pre-production batch of 15 used to test the design in actual squadron service. Mitsubishi

"Nell" bombers over China in the late 1940's.

engineers had been reluctant to clear these fighters for combat before they had been fully tested. Navy engineers differed; the Zero was so promising that they believed any changes could be handled in the combat zone, and technicians and engineers were sent along with the Zeros to make what ever modifications were found necessary after battle experience.

On 12 September, the Zeros were airborne again to escort 27 bombers over Chungking and back. The Japanese pilots were determined to fire their guns at the enemy even if they had to leave the bombers to do it. As the bomber force left the target area, the Zero pilots spotted what appeared as five enemy aircraft on the ground, and dived to attack. They proved to be decoys, but the Zeros shot up at will the Shihmachow Air Field and other ground installations. Their actions goaded the Chinese to come up and fight, but none rose to the challenge. Despite the lack of aerial opposition to the Zero, post-strike aerial photography taken by a Mitsubishi C5M ("Babs") reconnaissance aircraft confirmed the presence of 32 Chinese planes at dispersed locations around the city.

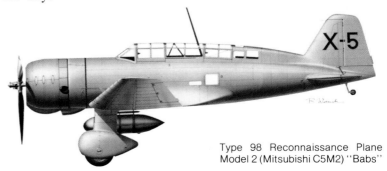

Type 98 Reconnaissance Plane
Model 2 (Mitsubishi C5M2) "Babs"

The situation changed, however, when the Zero's fourth mission was flown on 13 September. This became their day of "first blood," creating a legend that would build and remain throughout World War II and beyond. Once again, the Zeros were escorting the bomber force deep into mainland China for an attack on Chungking. As before, not one Chinese fighter rose to the attack and the Japanese bombs rained on the city.

As the attacking force left the target area, a lone Japanese reconnaissance plane high above the burning city spotted Chinese fighters converging over the area. Wasting no time, the observer reported this sighting to the departing formation of Zeros. Wheeling back toward the city and climbing for an advantage in altitude, Lieutenant Shindo led his squadron of Zeros in a classic situation of surprise and pounced on the unsuspecting Chinese pilots.

Polikarpov I-16/10

For the Chinese, a painful one-sided air duel took place. The Zeros swarmed over the startled enemy pilots, cutting their aircraft out of the sky with their machine-guns and cannon fire. The Russian-made Polikarpov I-15 biplanes and chunky I-16 monoplane fighters were totally outclassed by the swift and agile Zeros and within minutes plumes of smoke from falling Chinese planes filled the`sky. When the slaughter ended, all 27 Chinese fighters were destroyed. If there was any disappointment to the Japanese pilots, it was that a few enemy planes were not destroyed until they were landing, and one, in his effort to escape, crashed when flying too low to the ground, depriving the Japanese pilots of aerial targets. Not one Zero was lost in this opening air battle, which was the birthplace of an image of invincibility for the new fighter and the skill of its pilots.

With the threat of Zeros engaging any Chinese aircraft that might appear, twin-engined as well as single-engined Japanese bombers could attack at will with little threat of opposition. On 16 September, a single large Chinese aircraft of an unrecorded type was spotted over the city of Chungking and was immediately shot down by the six Zeros that were committed to strikes that day. This was the last mission flown in the month of September for these service test aircraft. For the remaining two weeks of that month, mechanics prepared the Zeros for the forthcoming flights that would take them even deeper into enemy territory where the Chinese had retreated.

When this small experimental force of Zero fighters was ready for more combat flying, they were sent on a very long-range mission against Chengtsu in Szechwan Province on 4 October, 1940. Twenty-seven bombers escorted by eight Zeros were to flush out the Chinese at this remote retreat.

The Model 11 Zero fighter, the first production version. This flight of two was

Again the attack was unchallenged. As the bombers departed the target area, the formation of Zeros broke off and circled back, undetected, in a wide arc above broken clouds. Bursting in among unsuspecting Chinese pilots flying at Taipingssu Air Field, they downed five Chinese I-16 fighters and one Russian-made Tupolev medium bomber before resorting to ground strafing attacks. Reconnaissance photos later confirmed as many as 19 aircraft of various types were destroyed on the ground. Only two Zeros received light damage.

From these encounters, the Chinese considered the Zero fighter to be invincible, and their pilots treated it with such caution that interceptions virtually came to an end. Thus, the Japanese gained air superiority over almost the entire Chinese theatre of war. This complete control of the air meant that bombers of all descriptions would be sent on operations deep into Chinese territory at will, protected by the awe-inspiring Zero. During the four months from 19 August, 1940, until the end of that year, a total of 153 Zero sorties were flown in 22 missions during which 59 Chinese aircraft were shot down and 101 destroyed on the ground without any loss in the Zero force.

From October, 1940, to April, 1941, the Mitsubishi G3M2 ("Nell") bomber squadrons were withdrawn from the mainland for reorganization. During this six-month period, the Zero was the only aircraft that could attack the Chinese on all fronts since they had retreated beyond the effective range of the single-engined Japanese Navy bombers and A5M4 ("Claude") fighters, and meanwhile the Zero pilots continued to taunt Chinese pilots into combat and maintaining their one-sided superiority.

part of a group of 15 first committed to combat over China.

The air war over China in the early part of 1941 followed consistently the events of 1940. By September that year, the Zeros had flown 354 sorties, shot down 44 enemy aircraft, damaged 62 more, and by now had lost two Zeros as a result of anti-aircraft fire. From this point, a number of air units were systematically withdrawn from the China front in preparation for an even greater conflict. For the Zero this air war over China had been decidedly a one-sided affair. As the opening of the Pacific war against the United States drew near, Japanese planners had unshaking faith in the ability of the Zero against the then existing American and British aircraft. A few recognized however that should such a war be prolonged, the Japanese and their Zero would face an array of weapons whose qualities and quantities could only be guessed at. The days of crushing superiority would be short lived.

Early Generations

When the Zero was in the design stage, its concept was far more advanced than any other carrier-borne fighter then in existence anywhere in the world, or in any stage of development at that time. To trace the historic development of the Zero, it is well to examine briefly the lineage of the five previous generations of operational carrier-borne fighters used by the Imperial Japanese Navy and their counterparts of other nations.

This line of fighters and other tactical aircraft began when aircraft carriers came into fleet use by the world's major naval powers in the early 1920s. The Japanese were first to complete and launch a true aircraft carrier, the *Hosho*. Completed in December, 1922, she was designed and built as a carrier from the keel up; in contrast, the later USS *Langley*, recommissioned in 1925, was a conversion from the USS *Jupiter*, a 1913 collier. During World War I the British had converted a battle-cruiser into HMS *Furious*, a hybrid carrier recommissioned as an aircraft carrier in 1925. In her 1917 configuration she had a limited flight deck area forward of the superstructure; aft, she kept her battle-cruiser armament.

In February, 1923, initial take offs and landings were made on the *Hosho* by Mitsubishi's British pilot Lieutenant William Jordan late of the Royal Flying Corps, flying one of the company's Type 10 Carrier-borne fighters.

Two years previously in January, 1921, a British Air Mission led by Captain Sir William Francis Sempill, RN, (Also known as Capt. The Master of Sempill) had been invited to Japan to advise the Imperial Japanese Navy on equipping and training its air arm. British Gloster Sparrowhawk fighters were selected as Japan's first carrier-borne fighters. Their design, of 1919–1920 vintage, was basically that of the Nieuport Nighthawk, modified and re-engined by the Gloucestershire Aircraft Co. Ltd. Fifty were purchased, and parts of 40 more were acquired. Most of the latter were assembled into complete aircraft by the Navy Arsenal at Yokosuka. Many of these lively Sparrowhawks powered by 230-hp Bentley B.R. 2 nine-cylinder rotary engines remained in service up to 1928.

As Japan embarked on its own aircraft industry, it was heavily influenced by foreign designs and designers. The Mitsubishi Internal Combustion Engine Manufacturing Co., located then in Kobe and beginning a new venture in manufacturing aircraft, employed the services of Herbert Smith, formerly with Sopwith as their chief designer. From this company came the first in a series of carrier-borne aircraft for various missions. Because of this engineering team leadership, the new fighter carried the influence seen in earlier Sopwith designs. Completed in October, 1921, these were identified as Type 10 Carrier-borne Fighters (signifying the 10th year of Emperor Taisho). These aircraft have the distinction of being the first fighters designed for carrier operation, while aircraft of other nations at that time were adaptations of existing land-based fighters. A total of 128 machines was produced, and they remained in service for nine

Type 10 Carrier-borne Fighter

years — until 1929, serving simultaneously with the Sparrowhawks. At the onset, the performance of the Type 10 Fighter, powered by the Mitsubishi-built Hispano-Suiza 300-hp engine, was comparable to, if not better than, that of other fighters operated from aircraft carriers of other nations of the world. Their greatest drawback was that they remained in service far too long.

The second generation of Japanese shipboard fighters which entered service in 1929 was also influenced by foreign design. This time the Nakajima Aircraft Company had won the competition with their license-built Gloster Gambet. This British design, stemming from the Gloster Grebe of 1923 vintage, became the Type 3 Carrier-borne Fighter (Type 3 identified the 3rd year of the Showa period – 1928). Unfortunately, this fighter design was already sadly outdated upon delivery. At the same time the US Navy was outfitting its three carriers with new Boeing F4B-1s, supplementing late model Curtiss F6C-3 fighters.

The type 3 Carrier-borne Fighters saw action during the Shanghai Incident and the initial stage of the Sino–Japanese Incident, but under the circumstances their obsolescence was not critical. These 420-hp, Jupiter-powered fighters served until 1935, their latter years in second line roles. Approximately 150 fighters of this type were manufactured by Nakajima.

For this time period, nearly all carrier based fighters were equipped with engines of the 400–500-hp range including the Nakajima Type 3 fighter. Although the Type 3 was an outdated design for worldwide front-line carrier fighters, it was the lightest and considered the most manoeuvrable. In combat, however, it would have lacked speed and firepower.

When Japan adopted a new designation system for its Navy aircraft in 1927, the Type 3 fighter was assigned the earliest designation in this system as A1N1. The "A" series signifies carrier-based fighter, first in the new designation series, while "N" shows this as having been designed by Nakajima. This closely resembles the U.S. Navy method of designations used from 1922 to 1963, an organizational system that Japan greatly admired.

As the Japanese aviation industry grew, they became less dependent on foreign designs, yet were not hesitant to use the best forms of technology found in foreign equipment and improve upon it. The third set of Japanese carrier-borne fighters to be selected in 1930 for its growing fleet, now containing three carriers, was the Nakajima Type 90, identified by the Japanese year 2590 (AD 1930). When these came off the production line in 1931, they were modern fighters by world standards. Japan had caught up. Production of 100 of these fighters rapidly replaced the two-year-old A1N1s which by now were actually outdated by eight years in comparable design technology. The design, although Japanese, was influenced by the Boeing Model 69B the export version of the F2B of which Japan had purchased one example in 1928. This very manoeuvrable Japanese fighter, designated A2N1 after it was accepted by the Navy, was powered by a Nakajima-built Bristol Jupiter engine, called the Kotobuki 2 generating 460 hp.

When the A2N1 entered service in 1932, its coun-terparts in the U.S. Navy were the all metal fuselage Boeing F4B-3s and -4s which remained front-line equipment for the next three years. On Great Britain's two carriers were the one-year-old sleek-lined Hawker Nimrod biplanes. This navalized and strengthened version of the RAF's Fury was highly regarded by pilots and had a long life with the Fleet Air Arm. Nimrods were powered by a 525-hp Rolls-Royce Kestrel inline engine which gave a very pleasing appearance to this fighter. In order to remain abreast of modern design trends, Japan succeeded in purchasing one Nimrod for study in 1934.

France was the fourth country to have an aircraft carrier prior to the birth of the Zero: the *Béarn*, launched in 1926. She carried French-built fighters throughout her career, parasol-wing designs that were adaptations of land-based aircraft. The threat of World War II prompted the order of American-made Grumman G-36A fighters (equivalent to F4F-3 model with Wright GR-1820 "Cyclone" engines) to replace the French-built designs, but France capitulated in 1940 before any of the American aircraft were delivered.

Japan held the biplane design for its fourth generation of carrier-borne fighters which began in the mid-1930s. This was a refinement of the A2N, Type 90, which became the Nakajima A4N, Type 95 fighter. These cleaner biplanes entered production in 1935 and 221 machines were delivered. A little faster than the A2N, the A4N was heavier, and not fully compensated for by the increase in power of the 670-hp *Hikari* engine, thus, pilots preferred the agility of the earlier model. This pilot preference would emerge again in a heated discussion over the design of the Zero when a choice in performance between speed and range became an issue. Due to the shorter range of the A4N, its activities were limited during the initial stage of the Sino–Japanese Incident. These were the last biplane fighters for the Imperial Japanese Navy.

Era of the Monoplanes

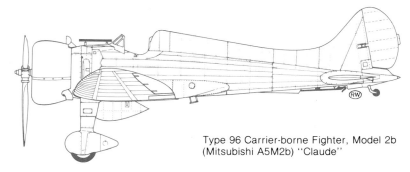

Type 96 Carrier-borne Fighter, Model 2b
(Mitsubishi A5M2b) "Claude"

It was at this point – the generation of Navy fighters preceding the Zero – that the Japanese not only equalled, but in some standards surpassed other nations in aircraft of this type. The new Mitsubishi Type 96 Carrier Fighter, having been designated A5M as a service aircraft, was the first of the low wing monoplanes for carrier duty, a configuration that all future designs would follow. A compromise had been made here, often with verbal objections by Navy pilots, for improving speed and range at some sacrifice to manoeuvrability by departing from the biplane arrangement. These monoplanes went into service on 18 September, 1937, and were soon

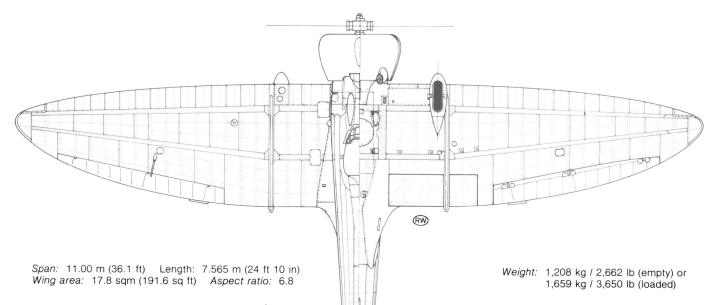

Span: 11.00 m (36.1 ft)   *Length:* 7.565 m (24 ft 10 in)
Wing area: 17.8 sqm (191.6 sq ft)   *Aspect ratio:* 6.8

Weight: 1,208 kg / 2,662 lb (empty) or
1,659 kg / 3,650 lb (loaded)

operating from the aircraft carrier *Kaga*. The A5M, later given the code name "Claude" by the Allies, arrived none too soon for the Japanese in the stiffening air war over China as the second Sino-Japanese conflict flared up again. Replacing obsolete A2N and A4N biplanes that were now being heavily mauled by Chinese fighters, they escorted bombing attacks over Nanking and other parts of the mainland of China, quickly gaining mastery of the air. They were a superior opponent to all aircraft types the Chinese could muster. The overall performance of these new all-metal monoplanes seemed ignored by other nations – perhaps not only because of Japan's apparent isolation from the rest of the world, but also because pilots at that time still clung to the biplane concept with emphasis on manoeuvrability. Continuing with this philosophy, the U.S. Navy carriers had, as standard equipment, Grumman's stubby F2F and F3F biplanes featuring a retractable landing gear. The British Fleet Air Arm was newly equipped in 1937 with Gloster Sea Gladiator fixed-gear biplanes. Their service life extended into the early war years until they were replaced by Grumman G-36A aircraft that were originally ordered by the French for the *Béarn*, and later by G-36 Martlets supplied under head-lease by the British.

The success of Mitsubishi's new fighter did not come without its failures in this attempt to use a monoplane configuration. In an effort to meet an earlier requirement of the Navy for a 7-*Shi* (1932) experimental fighter, little time was granted to Mitsubishi to perfect its design for a new low-wing carrier based monoplane before being pushed into premature production. Specifications issued by the Navy for the 7-*Shi* fighter left little latitude for designers based on current capabilities. Due to the engineering level of Japan's aviation industry, the undertaking was too advanced and the new test series of only two aircraft was an almost total failure.

When the specifications were issued that eventually became the A5M ("Claude") fighter, no mention was made of carrier-based equipment. Only five basic requirements for what was then known as the 9-*Shi* fighter were specified; speed, climb, fuel capacity, armament, and maximum wing span and length were given. This gave the Mitsubishi design team led by a young engineer named Jiro Horikoshi, more latitude in which to design a suitable aircraft. Given a freedom that he did not have on his first design attempt with the 7-*Shi*, Horikoshi was able to innovate. He was quoted later as saying: "Since each man, and the group as a whole, had benefited from the knowledge and experience of working on the 7-*Shi* fighter, I was able to incorporate into my new design several novel ideas which represented a marked change over former practices. I could determine without hesitation the general policy, the aircraft's basic configuration, and details of the design, and expect full support from every member of the team."

In the design concept of the new fighter, the thickness of both the wing and the fuselage were kept to a minimum. The landing gear remained fixed, but was streamlined to the greatest extent possible. Its length was shortened through the use of an inverted gull wing. Retractable landing gear was an essential feature on modern aircraft, yet

Engine: Kotobuki 3-Kai, rated at 600 hp for take-off,
dry weight 410 kg (902 lb)
Wing loading: 93.2 kg/sqm (19.1 lb/sq ft)
Power loading: 2.77 kg/hp (6.1 lb/hp)

Max speed: 219 kt (252 mph) at 2,100 m (6,890 ft)
Climb rate: 5,000 m (16,400 ft): 7 min 59 sec
Armament: 7.7 mm × 2 machine-guns,
30 kg (66 lb) bomb × 2.

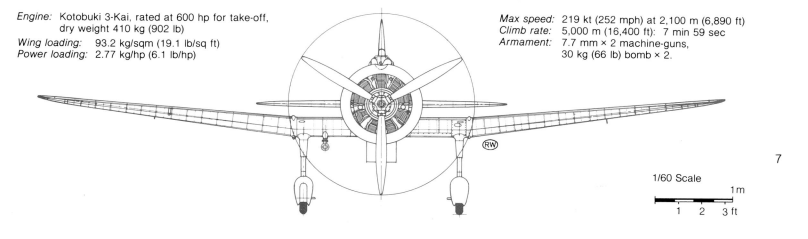

7

1/60 Scale

Horikoshi estimated that disadvantages in increased weight and mechanical linkage problems would not justify the speed increase. The fixed gear accounted for ten per cent of the minimum resistance of the entire aircraft; if retracted, it would only have given about three per cent increase in overall airspeed.

Great effort was given to perfecting flush riveting for the exterior skin of the airframe. This was an innovation just being introduced in German and American designs. Every consideration in streamlining was given careful study. When the structure was completed, skin crevices and irregularities were filled and painted to a smooth finish. Although a 218 mph maximum speed in level flight was called for in the design specification, the 9-*Shi* fighter reached 280 mph during initial tests. Powered by a 600-hp Nakajima *Kotobuki* 5 engine, its high speed was attributed to its very clean design, rather than an abundance of power.

Every weight-saving measure was also taken. Engineers concluded that even 90 to 110 pounds saved could affect the ultimate success in an air engagement. Horikoshi said, "The margin of 100 pounds between two opposing fighters was considered comparable with the difference between a veteran pilot and an unskilled novice. The fighter pilots compared themselves with the old *kendo* [Japanese fencing] champions, and asked for fighters with the quality of the master craftsman's Japanese swords. As a result of our pilot's figurative demand for the blades and arts of the old masters, the Japanese fighter planes were the lightest in weight and amongst the most manoeuvrable in the world. Our pilots sought tenaciously to master every trick of the superior fighter pilot, and they became well known for their prowess."

The delay between the final approval of the 9-*Shi* airframe and its acceptance as the Type 96 Carrier-borne Fighter A5M1 ("Claude") stemmed from the lack of a suitable engine. A number of radial engines and one inline engine, varying from 600 to 800 hp, were considered by the Navy. Finally, the 600-hp Nakajima *Kotobuki* 2-Kai-1, having the most reliability, was adopted for the initial production models. The gull wing was dropped in favour of a more conventional form to simplify production.

The performance of the early models was lower than that which was demonstrated by the prototypes, but they went into service anyway in the Sino-Japanese war which began in July, 1937. They became the backbone of the Imperial Japanese Navy's fighter force, and over 1,000 were built in several models. The model produced in greatest quantities was the A5M4 which remained in production at Mitsubishi's Nagoya plant until 1940. As power plants improved, these late models were equipped with the Nakajima *Kotobuki* 41 and 41 Kai engine, rated at 710 hp for take-off.

"Claude's" involvement in the Pacific War was very limited. With the exception of a token number used for the early attack against Davao in the Philippines, and again in the Aleutians, most of these open-cockpit, fixed-landing-gear fighters were retained in Japan by second-line and training units, giving way to its successor, the Zero Fighter.

The Zero is Born

At an earlier time, even while the A5M "Claude" was enjoying initial success as a combat aircraft in the conflict with China, the Imperial Japanese Navy recognized that the aircraft lacked range to escort the bombers to targets deep in the mainland. The aircraft would soon be obsolete compared to foreign equipment that was then being shown by potential enemy nations. From these elements developed new requirements by the Japanese Navy in 1937 for the 12-*Shi* fighter, the results of which became the Zero.

The study determined the requirements for a new-generation aircraft based on a number of situations, some hypothetical, others real. What was needed in a fighter operating over China in the existing situation was clear, but the requirements needed to combat an enemy which might materialize during the operational career of the aircraft took much planning. Not only was the theatre of operation to be taken into consideration in determining distances to be flown, but also the type and quality of opposition the enemy might have to offer. Considering all factors often called for aircraft with a performance reflecting technology that exceeded the actual capabilities of the aviation industry. Planners believed that the performance demands for the Zero were far in excess of the industry's capabilities to deliver; in spite of that, the Navy further increased the required performance of the proposed fighter.

Specifications submitted to Japan's aviation industry for the 12-*Shi* Carrier-borne Fighter were as follows:

Mission: A fighter capable of intercepting and destroying enemy attack bombers, and of serving as an escort fighter with combat performance greater than that of enemy interceptors.

Dimensions: Wing span less than 12 metres (39 ft 4 in).

Speed: Maximum speed exceeding 500 km/h (270 kt, 310.5 mph) at 4000 m (13,123 ft) in level flight. (*315.5 mph).

Climb: Climb to 3000 m (9,843 ft) within 3 min. 30 sec. (*3 min. 54 sec. achieved from takeoff start.)

Endurance: Normal flight duration of 1.2 to 1.5 hours with normal rated power (maximum continuous) at 3000 m (9,843 ft) fully loaded with auxiliary fuel tank; 1.5 to 2 hours at 3000 m (9,843 ft) using normal rated power, or 6 to 8 hours at maximum range cruising speed. (†10 hours, 18 gph, 115 kt at 12,000 ft, 1,700 to 1,850 rpm.)

Takeoff: Less than 70 m (229.7 ft) with head wind of 12 m/sec (43.2 km/h, 30 mph). Approximately 175 m (574 ft) in calm wind.

Landing speed: Less than 107 km/h (58 kt, 66.7 mph). (*55 mph)

Gliding descent/min: 210 m (690 ft) to 240 m (787).

Manoeuvrability: Equal or better than Type 96 Fighter A5M

Armament: Two Type 99, 20-mm cannon Mk.1, Model 3, and two Type 97, 7.7-mm machine guns.

Bombs: Two 30-kg (66-lb) bombs or two 60-kg (132-lb) bombs.

Radio: Type 96-ku-1 airborne radio and Type Ku-3 radio homer.

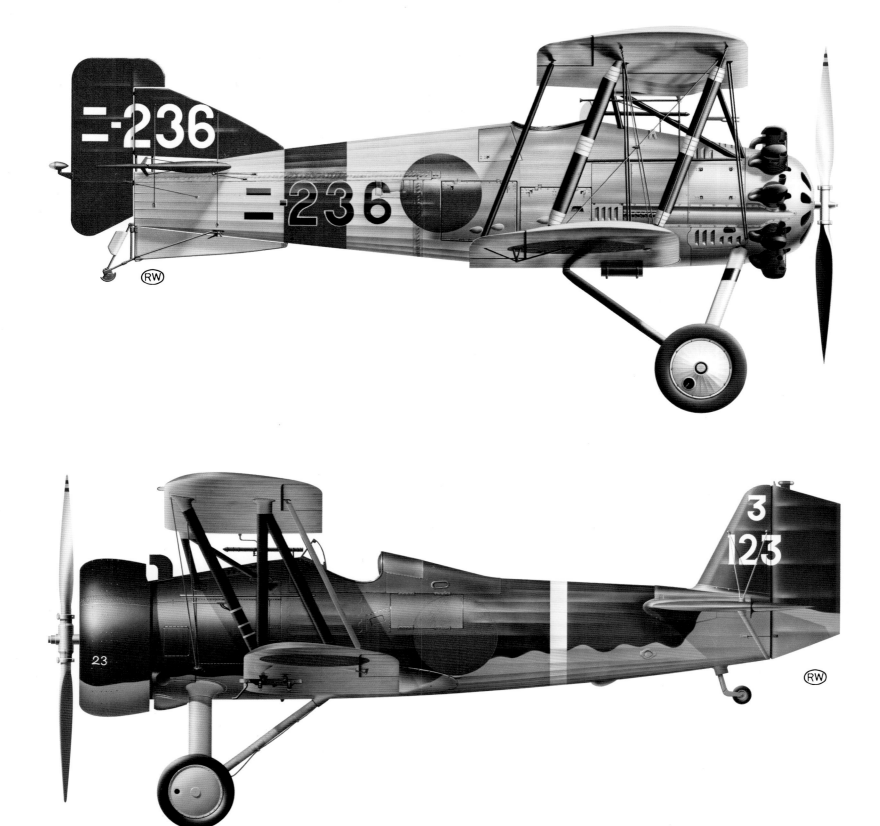

Nakajima Type 3, and Type 95

The license manufacture of the British Gloster Gambet by Nakajima as the Navy Type 3 Carrier-borne Fighter was characteristic of Japanese dependency on foreign designs in their early years of aviation. Light weight and maneuverable, the Type 3 was the best Japanese Navy fighter during the early 1930s. Equipped with two 7.7-mm machine-guns, these airplanes were used extensively during the Shanghai Incident in 1932 and performed well though limited opposition was encountered. They remained in first line service until 1935 despite their outdated design based on 1923 technology which stemmed from the early Gloster Grebe. Retroactively, when a new designation system was initiated by the Japanese Navy, Type 3

Fighters with 520 hp Jupiter VI engines became A1N1s, and 520 hp Kotobuki 2 powered models were the A1N2s.

As a successor to the Type 3, Nakajima produced the Type 90 Carrier-borne Fighter, A2N series. This 1930 design was developed in Japan but was influenced heavily by foreign technologies found on imported aircraft. They entered service in 1932. Nakajima refined the Type 90 design in 1935, which became the A4N, Type 95 Carrier-Borne Fighter (bottom). This model was a little faster with its 670 hp Hikari engine, than its predecessor, but its increased weight made it less maneuverable and it had shorter range. They too were armed with two 7.7-mm machine-guns. The A4Ns saw limited activity during the initial stage of the Sino-Japanese Incident and were the last biplane fighters for the Imperial Japanese Navy. About 221 were built by Nakajima.

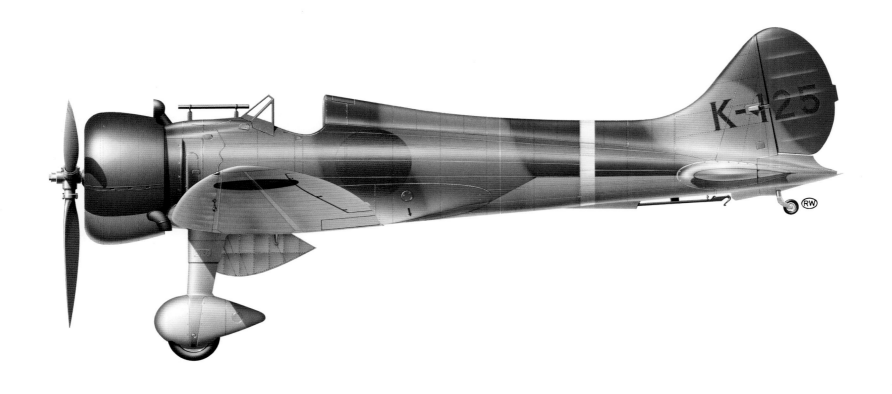

Mitsubishi Type 96

The Type 96 Fighter was the world's first operational low-wing carrier-borne fighter. Developed from the experimental Mitsubishi 9-*Shi* fighter with an inverted gull wing and remarkable performance, the design was simplified for production and military use. Drag was minimized by adopting an airframe of small cross-section with flush-riveted aluminum stressed-skin covering. Based upon combat experi-

ence gained over China, several models evolved over the three years of production that began in late 1936. Most noticable changes were the deeper looking fuselage and larger wheels and pants on later models. The Model 24 or A5M4 was built in larger numbers than any other variant of this fighter. When superseded by the Zero as a first-line air-craft, A5M4s, code named 'Claude' by the Allies, served as single-place fighter-trainers. A two-seat model was also built and used as an advanced trainer.

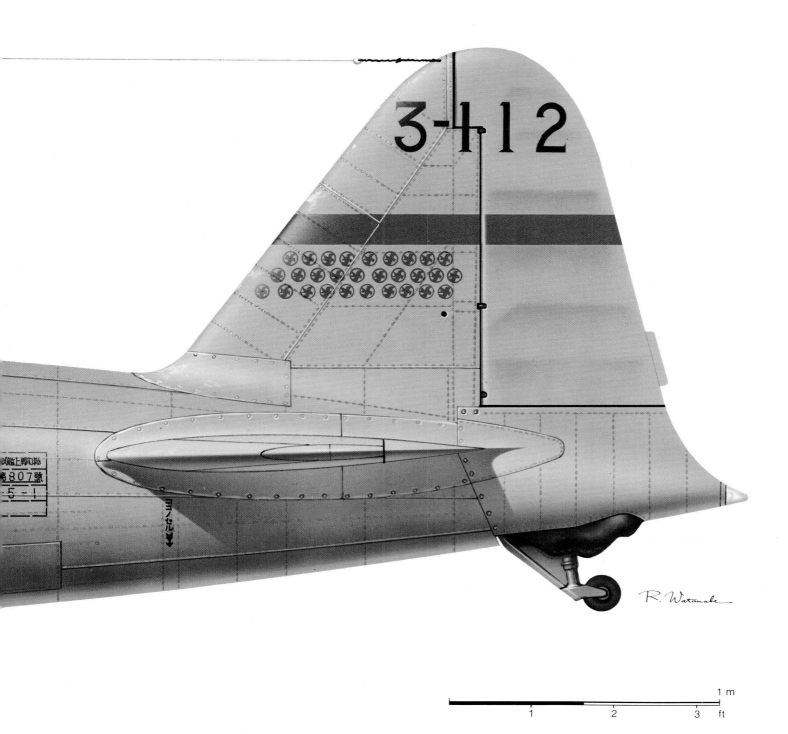

3-412

1 m

1   2   3 ft

R. Watanabe

pilots, but was also due to the limitations in horsepower that was available at that time. Performance was remarkable for only having a 950 hp Sakae engine, while opponents were above 1,000 hp and would soon reach 2,000 hp.

When the heavier armed and faster American fighters reached the combat zone, the frailties of the Zero became apparent. Armor plating for the pilot and protection for the fuel tanks had been sacrificed for lightness in the airframe. The only defense for the Zero was to outmaneuver the enemy during its many encounters with Allied fighters. Despite its weaknesses the Model 21 remained a lethal weapon in the hands of capable pilots in the early part of the Pacific War.

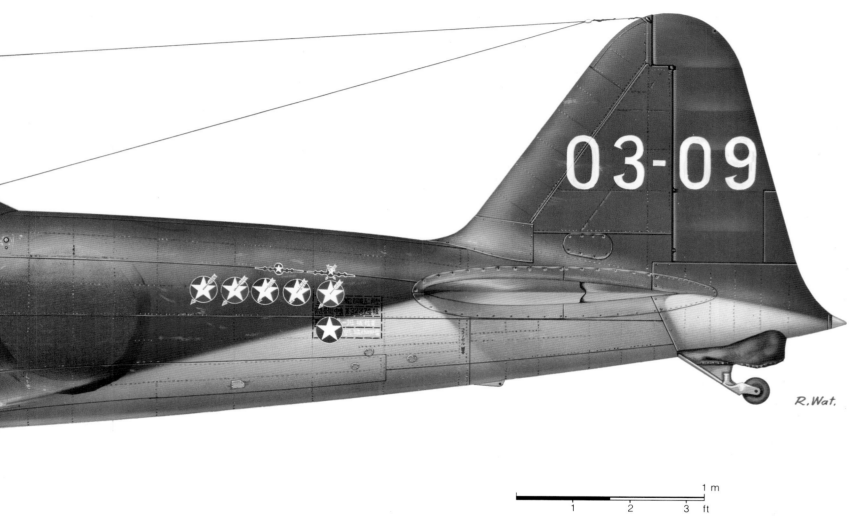

03-09

R.Wat.

1 m

1   2   3   ft

Mitsubishi Type 0, Model 52 (A6M5c)

In an attempt to keep abreast of newer Allied fighters, since a replacement for the Zero was not close at hand, the Model 52, A6M5, was developed. This version with a 1,100 hp Sakae engine incorporated jet-effect exhaust stacks and a new rounded wing tip with reduced wing span compared to the Model 21. When it entered combat in August, 1943, its improved performance was negated by the Grumman F6F Hellcat that entered service at the same time.

Continuing modifications were made in an effort to keep pace with the changing war situation. The Model 52a carried 25 more rounds for each of its two cannon and had thicker wing skin for improved diving speed. The Model 52b increased the size of one nose gun, added a bullet resistant windshield, and included a fire ex-

tinguisher system around the fuselage fuel tank. These additions were improved again in the Model 52c which also included two additional wing guns. With each succeeding model, engine horsepower was to increase, but this was very slight. With these changes to the Zero, dictated by the combat situation when there was little hope for more advanced fighter aircraft, the weight of late model Zeros had increased 1,050 lbs, or 28-percent, with engine power only increasing by 16-percent over that of the Model 21.

Despite these disadvantages, the Zero remained a deadly weapon in the hands of experienced pilots. However, by mid-1943, the loss of these seasoned veterans was severely felt by the Japanese Navy and the Zero was unable to be used to its fullest ability.

Mitsubishi Type 0, Model 21 (A6M2)

The Mitsubishi Zero became world famous from the opening day of the Pacific War and carried respect for its fighting capability to the very end of that conflict. It surprised the Allies with its very long range, strong fire power, maneuverability, and high rate of climb. It seemed to appear everwhere in large numbers on every fighting front —diving from the sun and firing its lethal 20-mm cannon in high speed attacks. Zeros first engaged in combat over China, and when the Pacific War began, the airplane was a proven weapon in the hands of veteran naval pilots.

Designed as a carrier-borne fighter it was exceptionally light weight compared to its combat opponents. This was not only neces- sary in order to provide the maneuverability that was demanded by its

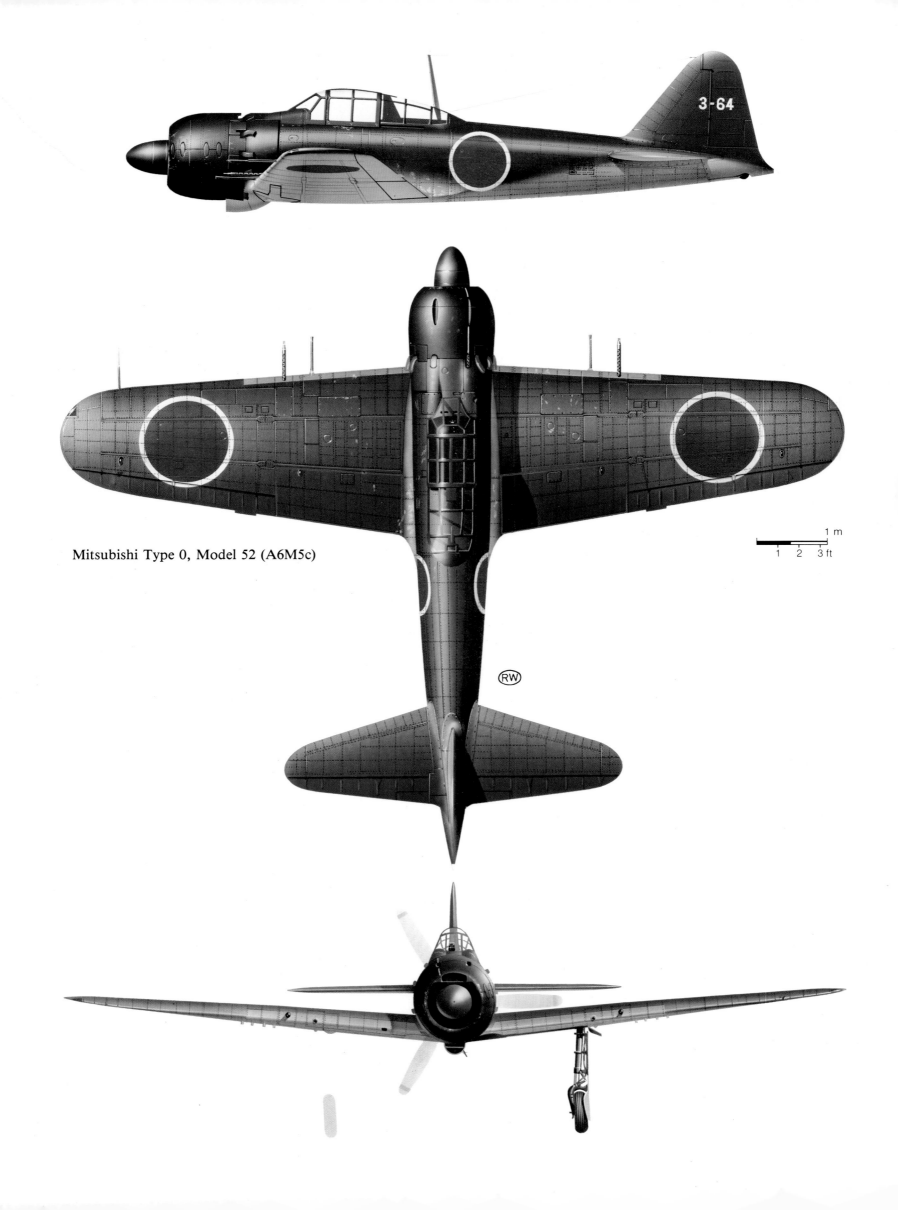

Mitsubishi Type 0, Model 52 (A6M5c)

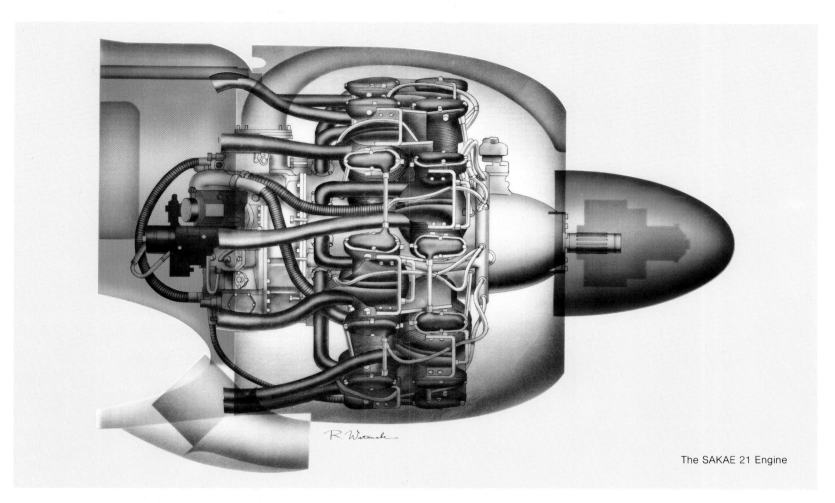

The SAKAE 21 Engine

Auxiliary equipment: Oxygen system, engine fire extenguisher, lighting equipment and standard aircraft and engine instruments. (It is interesting to note that specifications for the 12-*Shi* Carrier-borne Fighter had the same omissions of maximum weight restrictions, and carrier-borne operating equipment as the 9-*Shi* "Claude" fighter plus no mention of size restriction. Without these design limitations or requirements, the Zero was still to emerge as the best carrier-based fighter in the world.)

The requirements for this new fighter were revealed to representatives of Nakajima and Mitsubishi at a meeting held at the Naval Air Arsenal at Yokosuka on 17 January, 1938. Nakajima withdrew from the competition that seemingly posed impossible requirements. Mitsubishi was absorbed in the development of the Navy 11-*Shi* bomber and was hesitant to attempt an undertaking that showed little hope of success. The company was persuaded to accept the project however, in favour of not continuing with the 11-*Shi* bomber in spite of the risk of failure. With reluctance put aside, Jiro Horikoshi organized his design team to prepare for the new project as he did for the successful A5M "Claude." To assist him was a select staff of engineers, including Yoshitoshi Sone and Teruo Tojo for mathematical calculations; Sone and Yoshio Yoshikawa for structural work; Denichiro Inoue and Shotaro Tanaka for powerplant installation; Yoshimi Hatakenaka for armament and auxiliary equipment; and Sadahiko Kato and Takeyoshi Mori for landing gear and related equipment.

Note: *Based on US evaluation of captured A6M2, December, 1942.
†Performances recorded in flight by Saburo Sakai.

The immediate problem facing Horikoshi was the selection of the correct engine around which to design the airframe. A number of advanced engines were in the design and experimental stages, but to avoid the risk of failure caused by an unproven engine, the selection would be made from only existing and reliable engines. There were three possible choices: the 875-hp Mitsubishi *Zuisei* 13, the 950-hp Nakajima *Sakae* 12 and the 1,070-hp Mitsubishi *Kinsei* 46. The Mitsubishi design team did not favour the *Sakae*, at first, since it was produced by a competitor. Horikoshi favoured the larger and heavier, yet more powerful *Kinsei*, but with the Navy's insistence of a power loading not to exceed 5.5 lb/hp, the *Zuisei* 13 was selected and installed in the first two prototype aircrafts. This must have been an issue of frustration to this chief of design, for he was developing an aircraft expected to compete with a generation of potential enemy fighters that were already being fitted with engines over 1,000 hp, some of which were about to reach 2,000 hp. Beginning with the third prototype, the 950-hp *Sakae* 12 engine was installed which produced better performance than that with the Mitsubishi engine, and production of the new fighter began with this combination.

In order to achieve the performance demanded by the Navy, weight conservation was the prime order in the 12-*Shi* design. The wing, for instance, was built in one piece, thus eliminating heavy centre-section fittings for joining two halves. None of the structure in joining the wing had to be built into the fuselage, therefore these attachment fittings were kept very light.

A unique light weight material called Extra-Super Duralumin, E.S.D., was used extensively for the first time in

17

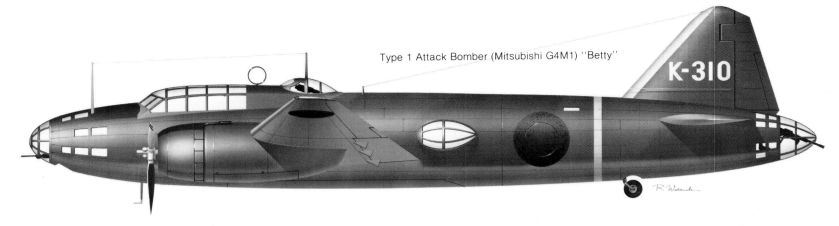

Type 1 Attack Bomber (Mitsubishi G4M1) "Betty"

K-310

this aircraft as a main part of the wing spar. This was very similar to 75S aluminium adapted several years later by the United States. This new alloy, manufactured by the Sumitomo Metal Industry, had a tensile strength 30 to 40 per cent higher than that of previously used Super Duralumin, comparable to 24S aluminium. Acquired from the manufacturer in the form of angle bar stock, it was then cut and milled to taper with the wing form and used for the main wing spar caps, creating a very light yet strong wing structure.

(After nearly 40 years, when examining aircraft of this type that survived, most of which are in the hands of museums, this E.S.D. material has crystallized in many places to the point that it can be scooped away with the blade of a screwdriver. This is the main deterrent in restoring Zeros and other Japanese aircraft that used this metal, for exhibit or flying today, but longevity to this extent was not a factor at the time of their manufacture.)

The design of the fuselage followed a non-standard method in another effort to save additional weight. The centre section was built integrally with the wing and, in fact, was not structurally complete until riveted to the top wing skin which forms the cockpit floor. Since the fuselage did not come free from the wing, it separated in two sections just aft of the wing trailing edge by removing a series of bolts joining the forward and aft fuselage sections at two fuselage ring formers. This avoided the awkwardness and impracticality of moving essentially a one-piece aircraft in restricted areas, and facilitated depot storage, as well as granting unobstructed access into the cockpit for major repairs. As can be seen, then, the entire design philosophy of the 12-*Shi* design team emphasized lightness, simplicity, and utility. This weight-saving design could indicate that the craft was flimsily built, but such was not the case. Its strength compared favourably with many American-built aircraft that were known for their durable structures.

Aerodynamically, the aircraft was designed for minimal drag, and good stability and control. A desire to reduce the wing loading below 105 kg/m² (21.5 lb/sq ft) for reasons of enhancing take-off, climb, and manoeuvrability characteristics resulted in the craft having a wing area of 22.44 m² (241.54 sq ft). The designers selected the wing airfoil section after carefully considering the desired mission requirement. This new airfoil became the Mitsubishi 118, with a similar mean camber line to that of a NACA 23012 series which offered minimal centre of pressure travel. Mitsubishi used this same refined airfoil with a great success on the G4M Navy Type 1 Attack-Bomber which became well known to the Allies as "Betty".

To prevent tip stall, the wing was given a 2½ degree washout angle which had also been used on the A5M "Claude". The tail surfaces of the Zero were designed to give exceptional longitudinal and directional stability characteristics.

Selecting the Armament

The purpose of any fighter aircraft is to provide a stable platform for a weapon system that can be placed in the best position to destroy the enemy. As the design of the Zero was evolved, these requirements were satisfied with a lightweight airframe to give it the manoeuvrability, and the optimum engine for pursuit. Selecting the best armament was the next consideration.

Throughout the world, there were several combinations of armament being considered during the time that the Zero was in the planning stage. For this period, around 1938, here is a sampling of these trends.

The Browning .30 calibre machine-gun had been the standard in the United States for a number of years, but the new generation of fighters was being armed with the large Browning .50 calibre machine-gun. Aircraft cannon were gaining popularity also at this time, but not to the extent of replacing machine-guns. When the Lockheed XP-38 prototype first appeared during this period, its nose contained a cluster of one 23 mm Madsen cannon and four .50 calibre machine-guns. Bell's new XP-39 Airacobra used its propeller drive shaft to house the cannon barrel for firing 37-mm projectiles, a feature which carried through to the P-63 King Cobra. Augmenting the one cannon of the Airacobra were two .50 calibre and two .30 calibre Browning machine-guns. The sole experimental XF4F-2 Wildcat was flying with four .50 calibre machine-guns; models so equipped would initially

slug it out with the Zero. Already well into production at this time was the Curtiss P-36 with the somewhat archaic firepower of one .30 calibre and one .50 calibre Browning machine-gun installed in the fuselage to fire through the propeller arc. The P-36 Hawk fighter was developed into the P-40 a few years later and armed then with four .50 calibre machine-guns to pit it against the Zero fighters.

The British had adopted the .303-in Browning machine-gun for most of its fighters at that time. The Hawker Hurricanes and Supermarine Spitfires which figured so prominently in the Battle of Britain in 1940 carried eight of these smaller calibre weapons so that more in number could be concentrated on the target.

The Germans on the other hand were relying on heavier weapons rather than quantity. Early production Messerschmitt Bf 109Es mounted four 7.9-mm MG 17 machine-guns, but later machines standardized on two MG 17s over the engine and two wing mounted 20-mm cannon.

Changes in weapon systems and combinations took place as these aircraft were advanced in different stages during the war. The trends were fairly well established however, and the designers of the Zero had to select and fit the best combination to their airframe. Their preceding design, the A5M "Claude," like all other Japanese service fighters of this period, was equipped with two 7.7-mm fixed weapons which were versions of the Vickers machine-gun. This weapon proved adequate for air combat over China for the opposition that was presented, but would be inadequate for the new 12-Shi Fighter.

A search had already started by the Technical Division of Japan's Naval Bureau of Aeronautics to find the most suitable armament for its next generation of fighters. One that brought the greatest interest was the Swiss 20-mm Oerlikon cannon, which was in use in several European air forces. One aircraft fitted with this gun was the French Dewoitine D.510, of which two were purchased by Japan in 1935 for close study and evaluation by the Japanese military and aviation industry. The major fault with this cannon, however, was its low muzzle velocity as compared to weapons of similar size. The advantages of the weapon, however, were its very low profile for installing in a wing, its light weight, and its ability to fire explosive shells. These features made it particularly attractive for fighter aircraft. When a determination was made that licence agreement could be acquired for the manufacture of

this cannon in Japan, it was adopted as the standard Japanese naval aircraft cannon, Type 99.

Manufacturers of the new licence built weapon became the Dai-Nihon Heiki Company, Ltd. (The Japan Munitions Company Ltd.) which also mass produced the ammunition. In time, six additional factories were set up, and by the end of the war, thirty-five thousand of these cannon had been produced.

Adapting this weapon into the 12-Shi Fighter design was not an arbitrary decision. The fighter specifications called for two Type 99 20-mm cannon. It was not an easy task to design a sturdy gun platform for this relatively heavy firing weapon to be installed into such a lightweight airframe. Horikoshi and his design team devoted considerable attention to this detail. When the initial design was completed, the Zero emerged with one of these 20-mm cannon in each wing just outboard of the landing gear, able to carry 60 rounds each. Augmenting the cannon were the tried and proven Type 97 7.7-mm machine guns; two were snugly fitted between the top of the engine and the cockpit.

Historians rightfully comment on the advanced performance qualities of the Zero when discussing its combat capabilities. Often overlooked however is credit for this selection of armament. The Type 99 cannon was a very large calibre weapon to be used by the Zero at this time when compared to the world standards already described. True, it did have shortcomings in low muzzle velocity and slow rate of fire, but reports of these cannon rounds hitting their targets and exploding brought a much higher total in kill records than if the lighter armament had been used as some proposed. The success of the new fighter was so profound when first introduced in combat over China, that Vice-Admiral Teijiro Toyota, Chief of Naval Bureau of Aeronautics, forwarded a letter of appreciation to not only the manufacturer of the airframe, Mitsubishi, and to Nakajima for the sound performance of the engine, but also to Dai Nihon Heiki for the effectiveness of the 20-mm cannon.

A6M5

R. Warmola

19

Design Uncertainties

There were times that uncertainties were raised concerning design philosophies being incorporated into the 12-*Shi* Fighter. The greatest controversy arose at a time when the prototype was nearly completed. Based on experience gained in combat over China, some navy planners felt that the new aircraft would fail to meet some of the requirements they thought to be necessary. To discuss these problems, a conference was held on 13 April, 1938, with all parties concerned.

Opening a major aspect of what turned into a debate was Lieutenant-Commander Minoru Genda, a highly respected combat leader, test pilot, and tactician. He held different opinions as to the course the future development of the fighter should take.

He argued that in a fighter, particularly a carrier-based fighter, the single most important characteristic is the ability of the aircraft to engage successfully in close-in fighting. Having this quality, the need for heavyweight cannon can be replaced by lighter guns and thus improve the aircraft's manoeuvrability. To further achieve this quality, a sacrifice of speed and range could also be made.

Opposing these views was Lieutenant-Commander Takeo Shibata, a man with equal qualifications, whose words carried the same authority as those of Genda. Shibata pointed out that Japanese Navy fighters were already superior in dogfighting performance to those of other nations of the world. Unfortunately, the air battles over China where fighter protection was needed to defend the bombers was taking place far beyond the range of Japan's fighters then in existence. Therefore, the next fighter must have not only long range but high speed as well. Even the slightest edge in speed would provide the margin needed to destroy the enemy. Shibata was convinced that the Japanese fighter pilots could be trained to maintain a clear superiority over enemy fighters, even with aircraft of inferior turning radius. To defend his theory he clearly pointed out that the maximum speed of an aircraft is strictly limited by its power and the design of the aircraft, a factor over which the pilot has no control. On the other hand, in dogfighting, pilot skill can compensate for any lack in manoeuvrability.

These arguments created much soul searching on the part of those responsible for the success of the new fighter. The conference was spilt without a decision since there were no grounds on which to challenge the wisdom of either man. To evade the stalemate, the Mitsubishi design team was asked to review the requirements set forth by the 12th *Kokutai* (Air Corps) that had a need for the new fighter in China, along with discussions just heard, and evaluate the embryonic 12-*Shi* Fighter with these demands in mind.

At this point, the new fighter was just a few weeks away from its maiden flight, yet at this moment it appeared on the brink of extinction. Horikoshi checked his earlier computations against the 12-*Shi* written specifications as well as the desires needed in the new fighter that were just debated. His findings were more convincing than before and once again he

The SAKAE 21 Engine (Nakajima NK1F)

14-cylinder twin-row radial,
fitted with two-speed supercharger.
Rated at 1,130 hp for take-off
1,100 hp at 2,850 m (9,350 ft) and
980 hp at 6,000 m (19,685 ft)
Maximum RPM: 2,700 rpm
Reduction gearing: 1:05833 (7/12)
Overall diameter: 1.150 m (3 ft 9 in)

submitted them to the Navy. With these facts he was quick to point out that the aircraft as requested by the 12th Air Corps would fail to match the overall efficiency of the aircraft already under construction. After fully supporting his case that the 12-*Shi* Fighter would possess not one or even two, but all three qualities asked for – superior speed, manoeuvrability, and range – the Navy relented and once again gave full support to the project.

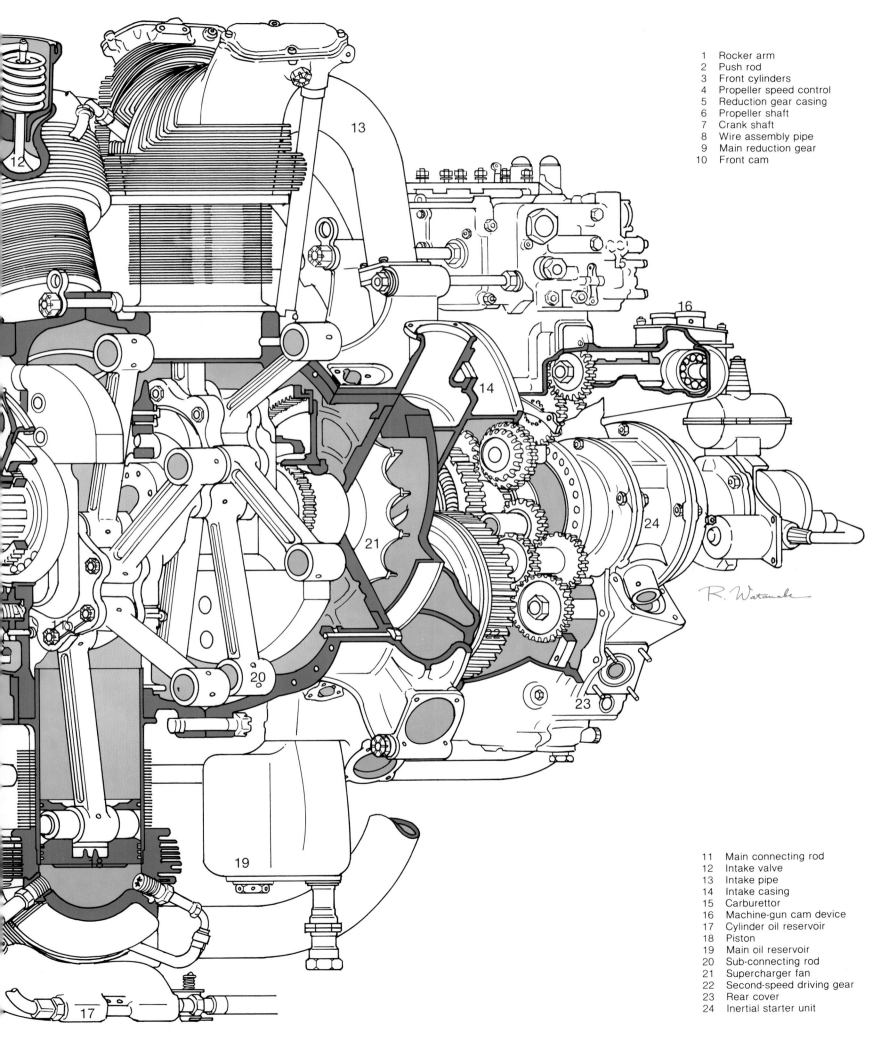

1 Rocker arm
2 Push rod
3 Front cylinders
4 Propeller speed control
5 Reduction gear casing
6 Propeller shaft
7 Crank shaft
8 Wire assembly pipe
9 Main reduction gear
10 Front cam

11 Main connecting rod
12 Intake valve
13 Intake pipe
14 Intake casing
15 Carburettor
16 Machine-gun cam device
17 Cylinder oil reservoir
18 Piston
19 Main oil reservoir
20 Sub-connecting rod
21 Supercharger fan
22 Second-speed driving gear
23 Rear cover
24 Inertial starter unit

R. Watanabe

The Prototype Zero

Model 21 (A6M2)

On 16 March, 1939, eleven months after the 12-*Shi* Carrier-Borne Fighter requirements were announced by the Navy, the first in this series was completed. Three days later, after weight and balance calculations were completed, and functional tests were run on the engine and other systems, the aircraft was ready to be moved to the flying field.

Partially due to poor planning, coupled with an aircraft industry that was a spin-off from factories established for the manufacture of other goods, few had adjacent runways. In the case of the Mitsubishi factory in southern Nagoya, the nearest suitable flying field was Kagamigahara Airfield, twenty-five miles to the north. The glistening new fighter, a product of the most advanced technology of its day, had to be disassembled and trundled to the airfield on two cumbersome, ox-drawn wagons.

The maiden flight of any new aircraft is a never-to-be-forgotten occasion, particularly for the men that created it. Zero designer Jiro Horikoshi reflected upon that day in April, 1939, as all concerned in building it waited for their machine to come to life.

"The long months of painstaking labour invested in the airframe, the wings, the engine, and the thousands of small parts all appeared in final form as a complete, but as yet inert machine. This silent machine was more than merely an assemblage of mechanical devices; the aircraft's sweeping, graceful curves expressed our attempt to master the air space which would be its medium. We hoped that our efforts would not have been in vain."

On that first afternoon in April, this "silent machine" did come to life as Mitsubishi's test pilot, Katsuzo Shima, signaled for engine start. When he was satisfied it was running properly, there was the routine of taxi tests to ensure that the brakes, controls and systems were working properly. Then with all eyes upon the shining fighter, Shima advanced the throttle, allowed the aircraft to roll forward, gaining speed until it was airborne. Assessment of control responses was quick and deliberate, and the power was reduced which allowed the aircraft to settle back on to the runway after a brief jump-flight. The Zero had taken wing for the first time.

In the days that followed, the tests became more extensive and more demanding. Aside from slight teething problems with the landing gear, a disturbing vibration persisted with each flight, for no apparent reason. Horikoshi felt that the two-bladed propeller was the cause of the vibration and substituted a three blade unit. Used for the first time on the 17 April flight, it almost entirely eliminated the vibration. This was also the first time that a constant speed propeller was used on a Japanese-made aircraft.

▲ A6M2 with light anti-personnel bombs (US Navy)

◄ Identification Plate Affixed inside Fuselage

(1) *Place of Manufacture:* Mitsubishi Heavy Industry Co., Nagoya Aircraft Factory.
(2) *Name:* Reishiki Type No. 1 Carrier-borne Fighter Plane, design 2.
(3) *Model:* A6M2   (4) *Motor:* Nakajima NK1 (   ) horsepower.
(5) *Manufacture Serial Number:* No.4593.   (6) *Net Weight:* 1715.0 kgs.
(7) *Load:* 650.3 kgs.   (8) *Weight, fully equipped:* 2365.3 kgs.
(9) *Date completed:* February 19, 1942.   (10) *Inspection mark:* 'Na-Ko.'

When all were satisfied that the 12-*Shi* Fighter had filled the Imperial Japanese Navy requirements, the first prototype was officially accepted on 14 September, 1939. Its military designation became A6M1 Type 0 Carrier-borne Fighter. The "0" was derived from the last number of the Japanese calendar year in which the aircraft would be placed into full service; 2600, equivalent to 1940. The alpha numeric designator A6M1 was seldom the identifier used by the Japanese, who preferred instead the term Type 0 Carrier-Borne Fighter. In the Japanese language, the words became *Rei Shiki Sento Ki* (Type Zero Fighter), often shortened to the abbreviation of Rei-sen or Reisen. Without question, this word identified the Mitsubishi fighter to every Japanese, but in this case, even for the Japanese after World War II, the most used name became "Zero-sen".

The entire and often changing designation system of Japanese Army and Navy aircraft was never fully understood by Allied intelligence during the war years. The inability to properly identify types made the task of defence difficult. To help solve the problem, a simple, easy to remember code-name system was developed. Male names were given to fighters, female names assigned to bombers. In the case of the Zero-sen, the name "Zeke" was applied, but by this time the term "Zero" was already popular and was more often used than "Zeke". In fact, the Zero became so well publicized at the opening phase of the war that even today people often identify nearly any low-wing radial-engined fighter having a Japanese insignia as a "Zero" – regardless of its type.

After the Navy took delivery of this first A6M1 the second prototype, which included among other things a correction in elevator control force, passed company testing and went into Navy hands on 25 October, 1939. The Navy was anxious to begin test firing the cannon system on this new fighter. Beginning in late October, the first firing mission scored nine hits out of twenty rounds fired in the first pass at a ground target 19 m (62.3 ft) square. Expectations of the Zero fighter were aroused even more by these rewarding results.

It is rare that all goes well continually with any new aircraft, and the Zero was no exception. On 11 March, 1940, test pilot Okuyama took off from Oppama Airfield in the A6M1 prototype No. 2 to investigate engine overspeeding during steep dives. On his second dive at about a 50-degree angle from 1500 m (4,920 ft) a loud engine roar at about 900 m (2,950 ft) was followed by an immediate explosion.

The Zero disintegrated instantly, and the pilot separated from the aircraft. His parachute opened, but at approximately 300 m (985 ft) the pilot's body slipped out of the harness and plunged into the sea. It was believed that Okuyama died in the explosion and that the parachute opened of its own accord.

The cause of the accident was never fully determined as there were a number of circumstantial possibilities. The most plausible cause was felt to be that the elevator mass-balance failed just prior to the accident, and during the dive and acceleration it is possible that elevator flutter started, causing severe vibration throughout the aircraft which led to complete disintegration.

The Tiger Unleashed

Despite this setback, production continued with only slight modifications becoming necessary as flight tests revealed them. On the last day of July, 1940, the Zero became a regular Navy service Type aircraft. Navy air force personnel at the China combat front heard about the outstanding performance of the Zero and asked for shipments of the new fighter at the earliest possible moment. As already described, 15 pre-production A6M2s were dispatched to Hankow in spite of cooling problems with the *Sakae* 12 engine. Technicians at Hankow corrected this problem and their solution appeared later on production aircraft. One that would not be solved until later was the frequent hang-up of the drop tank when pilots would attempt to jettison these expendable fuel tanks, especially at speeds of 207 mph or above. Pilots felt that their skill and their advantage in aircraft performance would outweigh the disadvantages in combat with the tanks still attached.

Historians have often said that the confidence gained by Japan with the outstanding success of the Zero fighter had much to do with initiating a war with the United States. Japanese intelligence and statisticians stated unequivocally that the superiority of the Zero fighter meant that, in battle, one Zero would be the equal of from two to five enemy fighter planes, depending on their type. Taking into consideration that the potential enemy had endless resources, Japanese victories had to be achieved quickly. The Zero would play an important part in achieving that goal by maintaining control of the air over any battle area. Because of this extreme confidence in the Zero, most Japanese Navy commanders were unshakable in their faith in victory for their planned military operations.

From the Zero's first day in combat over China, it was another sixteen months before the Zero fighter, along with Aichi D3A ("Val") dive-bombers and Nakajima B5N ("Kate") torpedo-bombers, slashed into their attack on Pearl

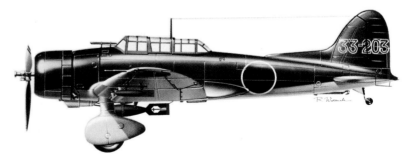

Type 99 Carrier-borne Bomber, Model 11 (Aichi D3A1) "Val"

Type 97 Carrier-borne Attack Bomber, Model 3 (Nakajima B5N2) "Kate"

Zero 21 taking off from carrier *Zuikaku* for the battle of Santa Cruz, 26 October, 1942.

Harbor. The allies were completely astonished at the sight of the new fighter and were totally unaware of the Zero's performance. Observers in China had submitted reports about the new aircraft but whether performance figures were exaggerated or not, these reports were thought to describe an aerodynamic impossibility and were filed away without further study or interest. The Japanese were equally surprised at Allied ignorance after having exposed their Zero for more than the year in the air battles over China.

The Zero left no doubt of its existence after its appearance at Pearl Harbor. Lack of knowledge and uncertainty of the potential of an unknown adversary creates a camp for fear, and from this the superiorities about the "won-der fighter" became wildly exaggerated. In an attempt to put down its true or mythical qualities, stories mushroomed that the sole genius of the Japanese was imitative. Early in the Pacific war, when the agile fighter was consistently victorious over obsolete US made equipment, the embarrassed U.S. authorities were quick to claim that it was merely a poor copy of this or that American design. Depending on the depth of the critic's aeronautical ignorance, the parent design was often claimed to have been based on Howard Hughes' racer or, the Vought V-143, which was bought by the Japanese in 1937. Once the Zero was accepted as a copy of American technology, it then became possible to speak highly of it.

Lieutenant Eijo Shingo, in command of carrier *Shokaku* fighter squadron, taking off in a *Zero 21* to attack *USS Enterprise*. 26 October, 1942.

Made In Japan

The Zero was, as we now know, a completely original design. No one will more vigorously defend this than the designer himself, Jiro Horikoshi. In his words, this is the response to this very old controversy:

"The Zero fighter was no more a copy than any other fighter used in the world today. All single-engined all-metal low-wing monoplanes are to some extent progressive 'copies' of the original Junkers 'Blechesel', the father of all these machines. There is a certain pool of common information from which all engineers draw. There is a certain reciprocal borrowing of detail ideas without permission during wartime, and by cross-licensing in times of peace.

"As virtually all competent aircraft designers will hold with me, the business of creating any new aircraft is a process of adapting the existing art and science to the problem at hand. For example, I will state that the undercarriage retraction on the Zero was inspired by the Vought 143, and that the system of fastening the engine cowl and the method of mounting the engine came from other foreign planes. And nothing else, so far as the airframe is concerned. It is no exaggeration to say that we did not look upon the general design or basic configuration of foreign aircraft with great respect. Any designer who fails, out of vanity, to adapt the best techniques available to him, fails his job. All engineers are influenced by their teachers, by their experience and by the constant stream of scientific information that is placed at their disposal.

"As foreigners inspected our aircraft in the combat zone, they were quick to identify accessories that looked familiar to them as copies of their own products. What they did overlook was that these were built under licence from abroad; wheels were manufactured by Okamoto Engineering Company under licence from Bendix and Palmer, instruments were built by the Tokyo Instrument Company under licence, or later in the war, by direct copy from Sperry, Pioneer and Kollsman. Sumitomo built hydromatic propellers under a licence from Hamilton Standard, as well as the German VDM propeller. The Nihon Musical Instrument. Co. built the Junkers and Schwarz propellers, while the Kokusai Aircraft Company built the French Ratier prop. We built 20-mm cannon licensed by Oerlikon of Switzerland and copies of the 13-mm (.50 cal.) Browning.

"I can claim, however, in the study of the Zero, its ancestors and descendants, that it was original to the same degree as other planes are, and that while it contains certain special features that were all its own, it serves as a prime example of a special design created to suit an unusual set of circumstances."

The Aleutian Zero Unmasked

Many months had passed in the war and little intelligence information about the Zero was in the hands of the Allies. Most of what was available was obtained from pilots that engaged the Zero in combat. Even line drawings showing the shape of the aircraft were misleading and highly inaccurate. It was essential that the Allies should obtain an intact Zero at the earliest moment for close examination and flight evaluation.

(National Archives)

That opportunity occurred during the diversionary attacks on Dutch Harbour in the Aleutian Islands during the Battle of Midway. On 3 June, 1942, Petty Officer Tadayoshi Koga's A6M2 engaged in an attack, developed engine trouble and was forced to make a landing on a remote clear area of Akutan Island. Landing with the gear down, the plane settled in the unexpected marsh surface and flipped on its back, killing the pilot. Little thought was given to retrieving this aircraft because of its inaccessibility until a U.S. Navy scouting party went to the crash site five weeks later and found the craft not too badly damaged.

(National Archives)

A captured Zero (A6M2) made ready for flight testing. (National Archives)

This Zero Model 21 was carefully removed and sent on a cargo vessel to the Assembly and Repair Department at NAS North Island, San Diego, arriving there in August, 1942. There, in a secure area of the blimp hangar, it was carefully inspected and repaired so that it could be flown for flight evaluation.

Major repairs were required for the tail, canopy and nose. The broken Sumitomo propeller was probably replaced with an American-made Hamilton Standard, for both were reported to be identical. This task of repair without technical data to work from was difficult, yet it was completed in early October the same year.

The mere gathering of flight data figures to be compared with similar data of another aircraft is often inconclusive since flight conditions are not always the same. A true test was to have both aircraft pitted together under the same set of circumstances. In order to do this, one of each American-type fighter was sent to San Diego for flight evaluation with the Zero. Army Air Forces pilots from the AAF Proving Ground Group at Eglin Field, Florida, brought an example of the Lockheed P-38F Lightning, Bell P-39D-1 Airacobra, Curtiss P-40F Warhawk, and the still very new North American P-51 Mustang. Navy pilots flew the Grumman F4F-4 Wildcat and an early model Vought F4U-1 Corsair for the tests. An intelligence summary of these findings, recorded in December, 1942, provides an excellent account of these comparisons. The often sought after results of this report are reproduced here in part for what is believed to be the first time in print:

P-38F Lightning vs Zero 21:

To begin this test, both ships took off in formation on a pre-arranged signal. The Zero left the ground first and was about 300 feet in the air before the P-38F was airborne. The Zero reached 5,000 feet about five seconds ahead of the Lightning. From an indicated speed of 200 mph (174 kts) the Lightning accelerated away from the Zero in straight and level flight quite rapidly. The Zero was superior to the P-38 in manoeuvrability at speeds below 300 mph (260 kts).

The planes returned to formation and both ships reduced to their best respective climbing speed. Upon signal the climb was started to 10,000 feet. Again the Zero was slightly superior in straight climbs reaching 10,000 feet about four seconds ahead of the P-38. Comparable accelerations and turns were tried with the same results.

In the climb from 15,000 feet to 20,000 feet, the P-38 started gaining at about 18,200 feet. At 20,000 feet the P-38 was superior to the Zero in all manoeuvres except slow speed turns. This advantage was maintained by the P-38 at all altitudes above 20,000 feet.

One manoeuvre in which the P-38 was superior to the Zero was a high speed reversal. It was impossible for the Zero to follow the P-38 in this manoeuvre at speeds above 300 mph (260 kts).

The test was continued to 25,000 and 30,000 feet. Due to the superior speed and climb of the P-38F at these altitudes, it could out manoeuvre the Zero by using these two advantages. The Zero was still superior in slow speed turns.

P-39D-1 Airacobra vs Zero 21:

Takeoff was accomplished in formation on signal to initiate a climb from sea level to 5,000 feet indicated. The P-39D-1 was drawing 3000 rpm and 70 inches manifold pressure on takeoff when the engine started to detonate, so manifold pressure was reduced to 52 inches. The Airacobra left the ground first and arrived at 5,000 feet indicated just as the Zero was passing 4,000 feet indicated. This manifold pressure of 52 inches could be maintained to 4,500 feet indicated. At 5,000 feet from a cruising speed of 230 mph (200 kts) indicated, the P-39 had a marked acceleration away from the Zero. Climb from 5,000 feet to 10,000 feet at the respective best climbing speeds, (thus eliminating zoom effect) the P-39 reached 10,000 feet approximately six seconds before the Zero. At 10,000 feet indicated, from a cruising speed of 220 mph (191 kts) indicated, the Airacobra still accelerated away from the Zero rapidly. Climbing from 10,000 feet to 15,000 feet, both aircrafts maintained equal rates of climb to 12,500 feet. Above this altitude the Zero walked away from the P-39.

Climb from 15,000 to 20,000 feet indicated, the Zero took immediate advantage and left the Airacobra. The climb from 20,000 feet to 25,000 feet was not completed as the P-39 was running low on fuel.

On a straight climb to altitude from takeoff under the same conditions as before, the Airacobra maintained the advantage of the climb until reaching 14,800 feet indicated. Above this altitude the P-39 was left behind reaching 25,000 feet indicated approximately 5 minutes behind the Zero. At 25,000 feet from a cruising speed of 180 mph (156 kts) indicated, the Zero accelerated away from the P-39 for three ship lengths. This lead was maintained by the Zero for one and a half minutes and it took the P-39D-1 another thirty seconds to gain a lead of one ship length.

P-51 Mustang vs Zero 21:

The P-51 was drawing 3,000 rpm and 43 inches manifold pressure for its takeoff and climb to 5,000 feet. The low manifold pressure was due to the setting on the automatic manifold pressure regulator. (This was the early Allison-powered Mustang.) The Zero left the ground and reached its best climb speed approximately six seconds before the P-51. It also reached 5,000 feet approximately six seconds before the Mustang. At 5,000 feet from a cruising speed of 250 mph (217 kts) indicated, the P-51 accelerated sharply away from the Zero.

Climb from 5,000 to 10,000, and from 10,000 to 15,000 feet produced the same results having the Zero accelerate away from the P-51 in rate of climb. At 10,000 feet from a cruising speed of 250 mph (217 kts) indicated, the Mustang moved sharply away from the Zero, and at 15,000 feet from a cruising speed of 240 mph (208 kts) indicated the P-51 had the advantage over the Zero, but slightly slower than at 5,000 and 10,000 feet.

The P-51 could dive away from the Zero at any time. During this test, the P-51's power plant failed to operate properly above 15,000 feet so the comparison was not continued above this altitude.

P-40F Warhawk vs Zero 21:

These tests were not completed with the P-40F because it was found impossible to obtain maximum engine operation.

[Author's note: An interesting observation on the foregoing accounts are the mechanical problems mentioned in this report which included one aborted flight, yet no problems were indicated with the Zero. Also of interest are the acceleration comparisons at altitude that were started at optimum airspeeds for the respective American fighters. The Zero being the older designed fighter, performed admirably.]

F4F-4 Wildcat vs Zero 21:

The Zero was superior to the F4F-4 in speed and climb at all altitudes above 1,000 feet, and was superior in service ceiling and range. Close to sea level, with the F4F-4 in neutral blower, the two planes were equal in level speed. In a dive, the two planes were equal with the exception that the Zero's engine cut out in pushovers. There was no comparison between the turning circles of the two aircraft due to the relative wing loadings and resultant low stalling speed of the Zero. In view of the foregoing, the F4F-4 type in combat with the Zero was basically dependent on mutual support, internal protection, and pull-outs or turns at high speeds where minimum radius is limited by structural or physiological effects of acceleration (assuming that the allowable acceleration on the F4F is greater than that of the Zero.) However, advantage should be taken where possible, of the superiority of the F4F in pushovers and rolls at high speed, or any combination of the two.

F4U-1 Corsair vs Zero 21:

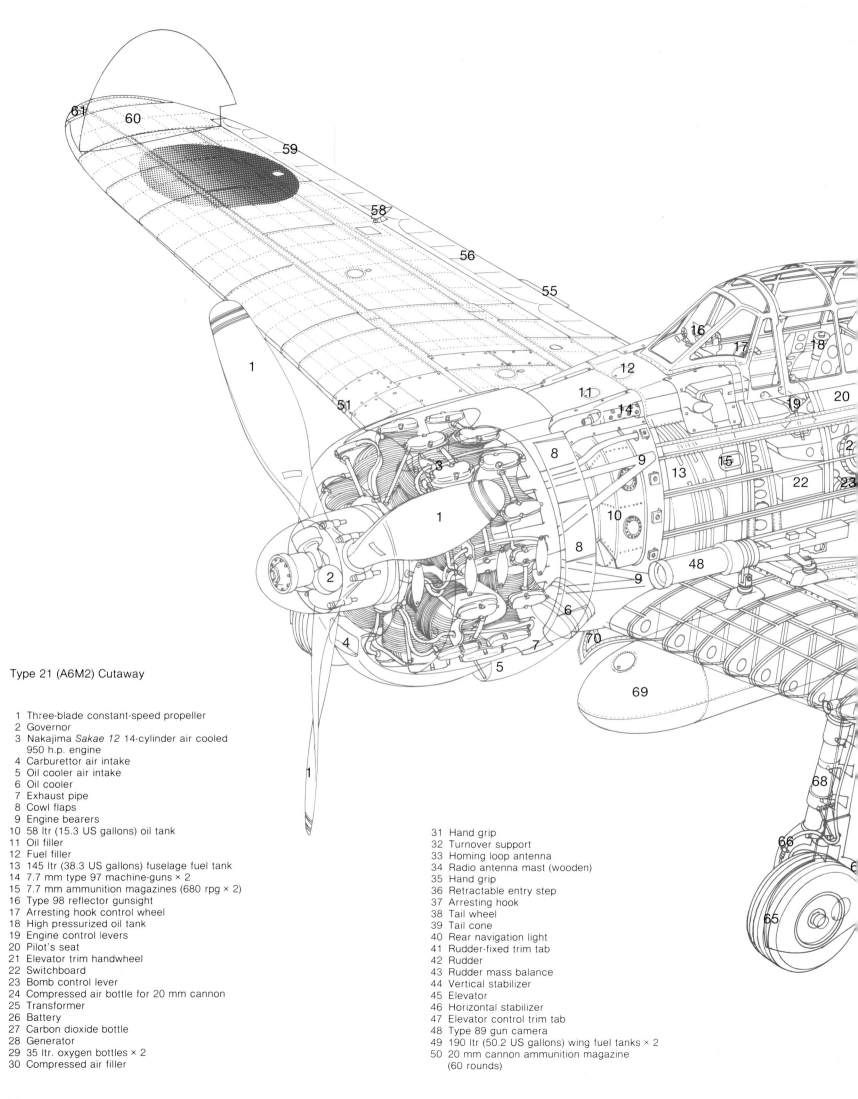

Type 21 (A6M2) Cutaway

1 Three-blade constant-speed propeller
2 Governor
3 Nakajima *Sakae 12* 14-cylinder air cooled
  950 h.p. engine
4 Carburettor air intake
5 Oil cooler air intake
6 Oil cooler
7 Exhaust pipe
8 Cowl flaps
9 Engine bearers
10 58 ltr (15.3 US gallons) oil tank
11 Oil filler
12 Fuel filler
13 145 ltr (38.3 US gallons) fuselage fuel tank
14 7.7 mm type 97 machine-guns × 2
15 7.7 mm ammunition magazines (680 rpg × 2)
16 Type 98 reflector gunsight
17 Arresting hook control wheel
18 High pressurized oil tank
19 Engine control levers
20 Pilot's seat
21 Elevator trim handwheel
22 Switchboard
23 Bomb control lever
24 Compressed air bottle for 20 mm cannon
25 Transformer
26 Battery
27 Carbon dioxide bottle
28 Generator
29 35 ltr. oxygen bottles × 2
30 Compressed air filler

31 Hand grip
32 Turnover support
33 Homing loop antenna
34 Radio antenna mast (wooden)
35 Hand grip
36 Retractable entry step
37 Arresting hook
38 Tail wheel
39 Tail cone
40 Rear navigation light
41 Rudder-fixed trim tab
42 Rudder
43 Rudder mass balance
44 Vertical stabilizer
45 Elevator
46 Horizontal stabilizer
47 Elevator control trim tab
48 Type 89 gun camera
49 190 ltr (50.2 US gallons) wing fuel tanks × 2
50 20 mm cannon ammunition magazine
   (60 rounds)

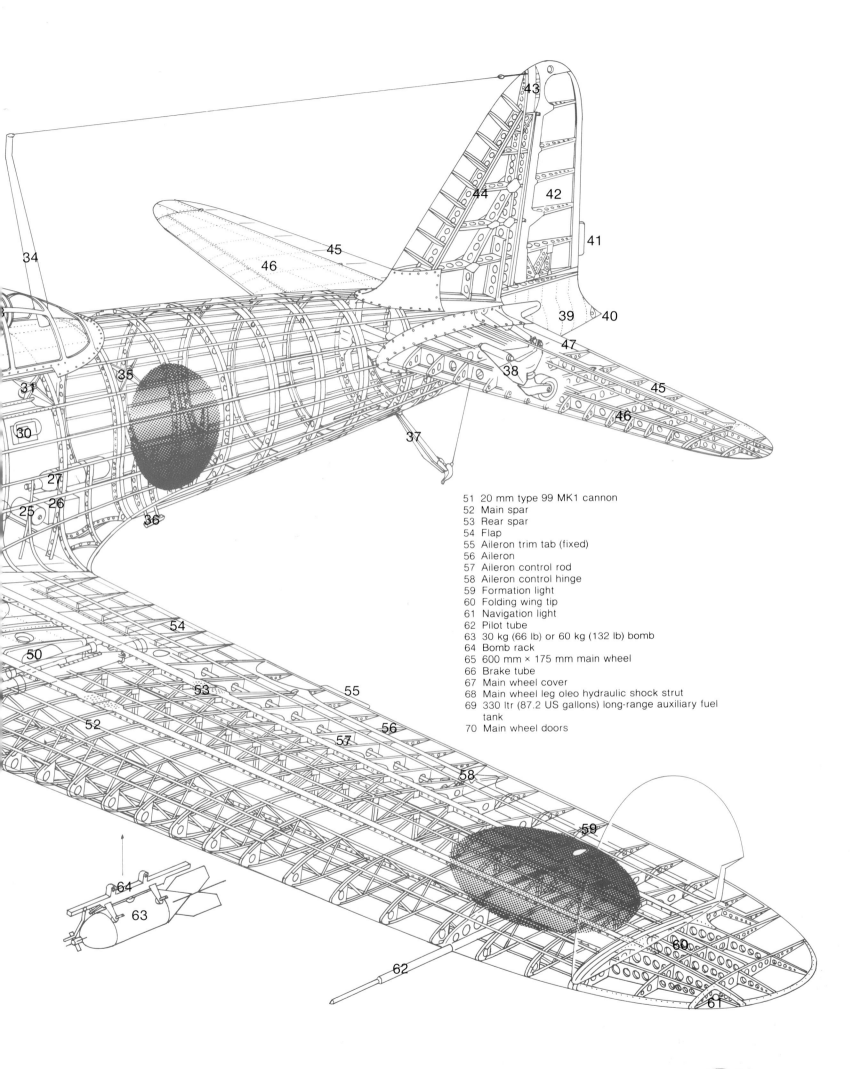

51 20 mm type 99 MK1 cannon
52 Main spar
53 Rear spar
54 Flap
55 Aileron trim tab (fixed)
56 Aileron
57 Aileron control rod
58 Aileron control hinge
59 Formation light
60 Folding wing tip
61 Navigation light
62 Pilot tube
63 30 kg (66 lb) or 60 kg (132 lb) bomb
64 Bomb rack
65 600 mm × 175 mm main wheel
66 Brake tube
67 Main wheel cover
68 Main wheel leg oleo hydraulic shock strut
69 330 ltr (87.2 US gallons) long-range auxiliary fuel
   tank
70 Main wheel doors

R. Watanabe

A captured Zero (A6M2) flying over San Diego area for testing, in early 1943.

(USAF)

The Zero was far inferior to the F4U-1 in level and diving speeds at all altitudes. It fell short in climbs starting at sea level, and also above 20,000 feet. Between 5,000 and 19,000 feet the situation varied. With slightly more than the normal fighter load, which may be distributed to give equal range and gun power, the Zero was slightly superior in average maximum rate of climb. This superiority became negligible at altitudes where carburettor air temperatures in the F4U were down to normal; close to the blower shift points it was more noticeable. However, the Zero could not stay with the Corsair in high speed climbs. The superiority of the F4U at 30,000 feet was very evident, and would persist when carrying heavier loads.

In combat with the Zero, the Corsair could take full advantage of its speed along with its ability to pushover and roll at high speed if surprised. Due to its much higher wing loading, the F4U had to avoid any attempt to turn with the Zero unless at high speed, and could expect the latter to outclimb the Corsair at moderate altitudes and low airspeeds. In this case, the F4U should be climbed at high airspeed and on a heading which would open the distance and prevent the Zero from reaching a favourable position for diving attacks. After reaching 19,000 to 20,000 feet, the Corsair had superior performance in climb and could choose its own position for attack.

During and after these tests, the first of subsequent Zeros to be captured and flown became an object of great curiosity. Charles A. Lindbergh is said to have been one of many noted airmen that were given a turn at flying this Zero. Several museums have since indicated that they possess this aircraft, but the truth is that prior to a routine flight at NAS North Island, in the summer of 1944, the pilot of a Curtiss SB2C Helldiver inadvertently taxied into it and chopped it to pieces from the tail to the cockpit. The Zero was a total loss.

The Zero Matures

As a war situation changes, so must combat aircraft be changed to adapt to the new environment and take advantage of advances in technology until fully replaced by new aircraft designs. In the case of the Zero, the Japanese Navy failed to substantially introduce an improved replacement for the Zero, to match the speed, armament and protection of the modern Allied fighters which began arriving in the Pacific in late 1942. Consequently, the Zero faced an even more potent enemy having both quantity and quality in its aircraft, while the Japanese pilots were left to rely on an array of improvements made to the Zeros basic 1939 vintage design. Its obsolescence could no longer be shielded through these modifications after 1943 yet, by necessity, it was kept in production until the surrender of Japan. As a consequence of being the first-line fighter of the Japanese Navy throughout the entire Pacific war, more Zeros were built than any other type of Japanese aircraft.

The life span of the Zero ranged from the superiority it enjoyed over China and the first year of the Pacific war, to the final desperate attempts to ward off swarms of Allied carrier based aircraft and the B-29s over the home islands of Japan. By examining each modification made to the Zero over this time period, it becomes clearly evident that the trend changed from being the aggressor to the defender. These changes in themselves encapsulate the history of the Zero, and in a way, the Pacific war itself.

As each of the Zero models is described, it may appear that a duel system of identification had been used; one being an alpha-numeric system closely resembling a method used by the U.S. Navy up until 1963, the other having the name of an aircraft followed by two digits. In fact, two distinct systems did exist. Officially, both were used by the Japanese Navy, but of the two, the use of its name designator was more commonly used.

With the letter system, the first letter identifies the aircraft mission. For the A6M5 Zero, a carrier-borne fighter, "A" signifies the naval mission. The 6 shows it to be the sixth basic design in the carrier-borne fighter series. "M" is for Mitsubishi, the design company, and the last number represents the modification number after initial acceptance of the design. This system was seldom used publicly since it revealed too much information about the aircraft in relation to other models in the Japanese Navy.

The two digit system that followed the aircraft name such as Zero 21 or Reisen 21, identifies the aircraft model. This designation is actually two numbers, not one double digit number as it appears, and is expressed as Zero Two-One. The first of the two numbers relate to the basic airframe and subsequent changes which are numbered consecutively. The second number identified the engine type changes made after the basic design acceptance by the Navy.

Mitsubishi 12-Shi, A6M1:

When the Imperial Japanese Navy accepted the 12-Shi fighter in September, 1939, it was assigned the designation A6M1. It is believed that this designation applied only to the first two prototypes since both were powered by the 875 hp Mitsubishi *Zuisei* 13 engine, and it was from the evaluation of this configured model that the aircraft was accepted by the Navy and given this Navy designator.

Zero 11, A6M2:

The third prototype was powered by the more powerful 950 hp Nakajima *Sakae* 12 engine which gave it improved performance and production status. It was the model that first saw combat in China; 64 were built, commencing in December, 1939.

Zero 21, A6M2:

Service test model 11's proved the effectiveness of the design. The Zero performed well aboard Japan's aircraft carriers, but their snug fit while riding on the elevators between the flight and hangar decks put them in danger of damaging their wing tips. To solve the problems, the wing tip sections were made to be folded manually, reducing the span by 500 mm (20 in) on each side for added elevator clearance. This structural change warranted a new designation, making this Zero, Model 21. Had the entire wing been made to fold to save space like that of the Wildcat, Hellcat and others of the U.S. Navy, it would have increased the weight in the structure, a penalty that the Japanese did not want to pay.

With this model, Nakajima Aircraft Company also began manufacturing the Zero in November, 1941, and together with Mitsubishi produced 740 of this type. Beginning with the 127th aircraft, a new balance tab arrangement was installed on the ailerons. The amount of tab action was linked to the landing gear retraction system. This reduced the required stick force that was needed for lateral manoeuvrability during high speed flight, yet provided responsive ailerons while at traffic pattern speeds.

By now, the Allies had learned the meaning of the model designation system used by the Japanese Navy, so the Allies referred to this Zero with its code name as "Zeke 21."

Zero 32, A6M3:

To compete with the expected increase performance in allied fighter aircraft, it was necessary to improve the Zero's altitude and climb performance. This brought about the most apparent design change in the basic appearance of the Zero.

Additional power was given to the Zero in the form of the new *Sakae* 21 engine with its increased output of 1,100 hp. This engine had a change in reduction gearing, allowed for a larger propeller, and incorporated a two speed supercharger for improved high altitude performance. The most visible feature in this engine change was the placement of the air-scoop for its down draft carburettor at the top front of the cowling and the nose guns firing out closer to the front of the cowling rather than along gun troughs at the top of the cowling. This engine change alone accounted for most of the 280 pound weight increase over the earlier Model 21. Fuel quantity was reduced by approximately 21 U.S. gallons due to the increase in dimensional size of the engine as a measure to retain the original overall fuselage length. Although the difference in fuel consumption of the *Sakae* 21 compared to the *Sakae* 12 was negligible in normal cruise performance, the tactical combat radius of the Model 32 was reduced considerably because of the difference in fuel capacity and fuel consumption at full power.

Despite this increase in power for the Zero, the performance anticipated to be gained by the designers did not materialize. Pilots flying the test models recommended removing the folding wing tips entirely, which was done, and a fairing was added to cover the exposed end. This brought some loss in overall performance but did provide the increase in maximum speed. With a shorter aileron that was necessitated by removing the wing tip, the two-speed ratio aileron tab arrangement was eliminated which simplified production.

When this squared off wing model was first encountered by the Allies in October, 1942, over the Solomon Islands, it was thought to be a new Japanese fighter. It was given the Allied code name "Hap" in honour of General "Hap" Arnold of the Air Force, but when Arnold found out about the name he was less than flattered and it was recoded to "Hamp". When the first close inspection of this type was conducted by the Americans on New Guinea in December, 1942, they discovered it to be a modification of the basic Zero form, and the code name was changed to "Zeke" 32.

The reduction in wing area by just over nine square feet gave slightly improved manoeuvrability at high speeds. This had been a shortcoming in the earlier configurations. Ammunition for the 20-mm cannon was increased from 60 to 100 rounds per gun. From production which started in July, 1941, 343 machines were delivered to the Japanese Navy.

Type 98 Reflector Gunsight

increase was due to a small fuel tank outboard of the main fuel cell in each wing which provided for an additional total of 24 U.S. gallons. This gave the Model 22 the longest range of all models, about 100 miles more than that which the astonishing Model 21 had tactically demonstrated. By August, 1942, this increase in the Zero's range was necessitated when required to fly as far as 560 nautical miles (644 statute miles) from Rabaul to the combat area over Guadalcanal. There they engaged the numerically superior and more modern allied aircraft such as the Vought F4U-1 Corsair, Lockheed P-38 Lightning and Supermarine Spitfire, and suffered heavy losses in this campaign.

When the earlier Type 99 Mark 1 Oerlikon wing cannons were changed in favour of the higher muzzle velocity, longer barrel Type 99, Mark 2, Model 3 cannons, this Zero became the Model 22a. A small number of Model 22s were operationally tested at Rabaul with wing-mounted experimental 30-mm cannon.

Zero Model 32, A6M4:

The assignment of this designation to a model of the Zero had been questionable for a long period of time since there was no record of its use. The Japanese use the number "4" with the same reservations that Westerners treat the number "13", and therefore it was presumed not to have been used for this reason although not avoided in numbering systems for other aircraft. (The number "4" which is *shi* in Japanese also has the meaning of the word "death.") It was not until 1968 that Horikoshi revealed that a Model 32 was equipped with an experimental turbo-supercharged engine, and this designation A6M4 was reserved for this configured model had it gone into production.

Zero Model 52, A6M5:

Despite promises in 1943 of a new interceptor that later was known to the Allies as "Jack," production as well as development lagged far behind. Again it became necessary to modify the existing Zero fighter in an attempt to counter the new American fighters which in many respects now clearly out-performed the earlier Zero models.

This new Zero Model 52 was an effort to simplify and speed production, as well as to increase the diving speed. Once again, effort was directed at redesigning the wing tip. The wing span remained the same as with the squared off tip, Model 32, but modifications included the elimination of the unused wing tip folding mechanism which was merely faired over, and rounding off the otherwise square wing tip. This not only simplified production, but saved weight although an overall increase of 150 to 170 pounds (68–78 kg) over the Zero 32 was experienced. For gaining the needed increase in diving speed, heavier gauge wing skin allowed this airspeed to be moved up to 355 knots (410 mph).

Another measure taken to improve speed performance was to replace the exhaust collector ring with straight individual stacks. This change directed the high velocity exhaust gas backward for additional thrust. These changes produced a Zero having a maximum speed which reached 305 knots (351 mph) in level flight at 6,000 m (19,700 ft), and

Zero Model 22, A6M3:

This reversal in a portion of the model number was a result of adding once again the round wing tip which matched the airframe of the earlier Model 21, yet retaining the larger *Sakae* 21 engine. The reason for this reversal was to gain back the loss in range which was partly a result of the decreased wing area. This aircraft actually preceded the square wing Model 32 in design concept but was presumably set aside to meet the request to eliminate the folding portion of the wing tip. By the time the Model 22 reached the production stage, the next generation, Zero 52, was rapidly approaching operational status. Therefore Zero 22, which appeared in combat after Model 32s, had a relatively short operational life despite the fact that 560 of this type were manufactured. They first appeared in combat in late 1942 when they were rushed to Buna, on New Guinea, and Buka, in the Solomon Islands where they frequently provided escort cover for vessels operating between the fighting on Guadalcanal and the northern supply bases.

This return of the "round-wing" model made a net weight increase of 123 pounds over the Zero 32. Some of this

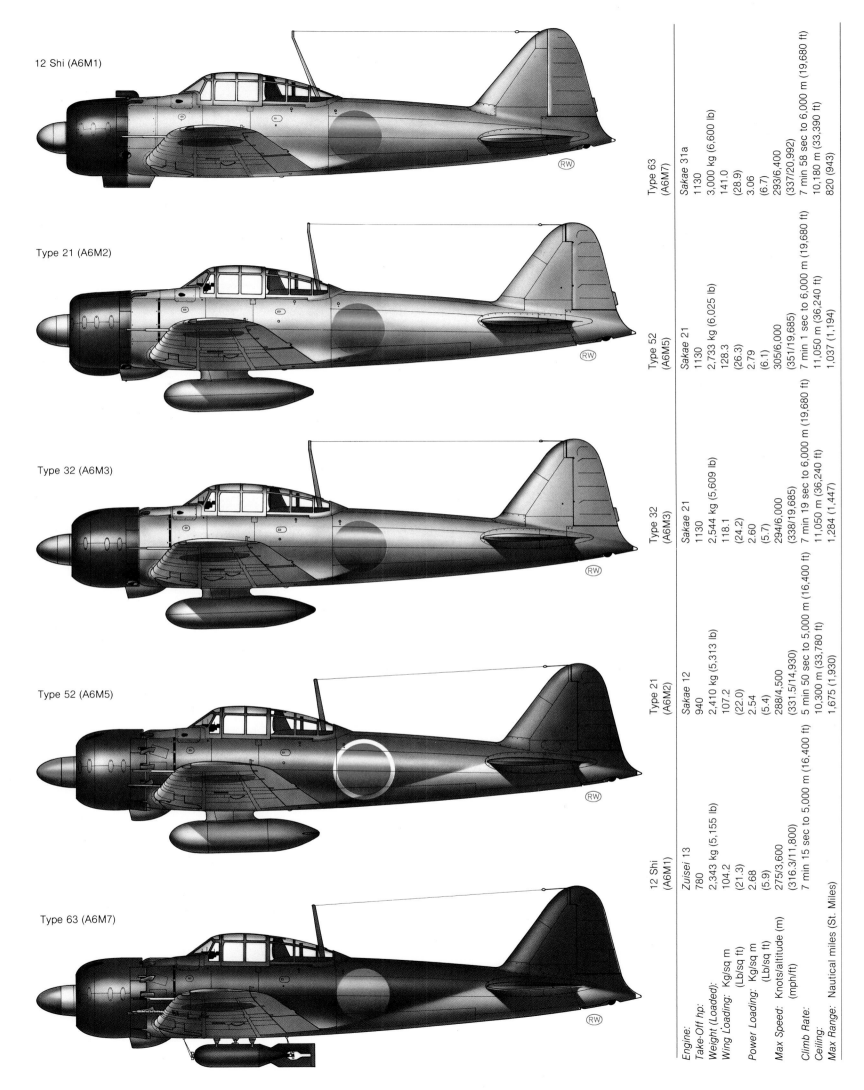

12 Shi (A6M1)

Type 21 (A6M2)

Type 32 (A6M3)

Type 52 (A6M5)

Type 63 (A6M7)

	12 Shi (A6M1)	Type 21 (A6M2)	Type 32 (A6M3)	Type 52 (A6M5)	Type 63 (A6M7)
Engine:	Zuisei 13	Sakae 12	Sakae 21	Sakae 21	Sakae 31a
Take-Off hp:	780	940	1130	1130	1130
Weight (Loaded):	2,343 kg (5,155 lb)	2,410 kg (5,313 lb)	2,544 kg (5,609 lb)	2,733 kg (6,025 lb)	3,000 kg (6,600 lb)
Wing Loading: Kg/sq m	104.2	107.2	118.1	128.3	141.0
(Lb/sq ft)	(21.3)	(22.0)	(24.2)	(26.3)	(28.9)
Power Loading: Kg/sq m	2.68	2.54	2.60	2.79	3.06
(Lb/sq ft)	(5.9)	(5.4)	(5.7)	(6.1)	(6.7)
Max Speed: Knots/altitude (m)	275/3,600	288/4,500	294/6,000	305/6,000	293/6,400
(mph/ft)	(316.3/11,800)	(331.5/14,930)	(338/19,685)	(351/19,685)	(337/20,992)
Climb Rate:	7 min 15 sec to 5,000 m (16,400 ft)	5 min 50 sec to 5,000 m (16,400 ft)	7 min 19 sec to 6,000 m (19,680 ft)	7 min 1 sec to 6,000 m (19,680 ft)	7 min 58 sec to 6,000 m (19,680 ft)
Ceiling:		10,300 m (33,780 ft)	11,050 m (36,240 ft)	11,050 m (36,240 ft)	10,180 m (33,390 ft)
Max Range: Nautical miles (St. Miles)		1,675 (1,930)	1,284 (1,447)	1,037 (1,194)	820 (943)

Zero fighters (Type 21/22) of the First Naval Air Corps prepare to take off from Rabaul in support of 'Operation *Ro-Go*.' November, 1943.

clearly improved rate of climb. This became the most widely used model of the Zero series with 1,701 manufactured, beginning in the summer of 1943.

This new model was pressed into service in the fall of 1943 in time to meet the initial appearance of the new Grumman F6F Hellcat. The Zero 52 could hold its own in performance against the slightly less manoeuvrable Hellcat, but the Zero was too often the victim of the heavier armament of the F6F due to its lighter construction and inadequate protection.

Zero 52a, A6M5a:

Within the Zero Model 52 series, three sub series followed. By the fall of 1943, the Zero Model 52a emerged with additional firepower that was now needed to encounter the Hellcat. This was effected by using a belt feed rather than a drum whereby the ammunition supply could be increased for each wing cannon from 100 to 125 rounds each.

To again improve the diving speed a partial increase in wing skin was made at high stress locations. This raised the maximum speed limitation from 355 kts (410 mph) to 400 kts (460 mph). Engineers were hesitant to push the limit beyond this point, but this did close the speed margin between 17 to 26 kts (20 to 30 mph) short of the diving limitations of the heavier F4U Corsair.

Zero Model 52b, A6M5b:

Some of the harsh lessons learned in combat with the lack of pilot and aircraft protection were applied to this model of the Zero. To fill the gap while waiting for the next generation of fighters to replace the Zero design, a study was begun in early 1944 to add protection features to the Zero. These began emerging in the Zero 52b. Most significant was the use of an automatic CO_2 fire extinguisher system built into the fuel tank areas of the fuselage and around the engine fire wall. For the pilot, a 50 mm (2 in) bullet resistant windshield was provided which consisted of two plates of glass with clear

plastic sandwiched between. For increasing firepower, one of the two fuselage mounted Type 97, 7.7-mm machine-guns was replaced by a larger Type 3, 13-mm machine-gun, the first change in armament size since the first prototype of the Zero.

This added fire power and improved survivability was in preparation for the pending battle of the Philippines which took place beginning 19 June, 1944. Mitsubishi turned out 470 of this model and Nakajima an unknown quantity.

Zero Model 52c, A6M5c

Every attempt was being made to maintain the survivability of the Zero which was destined to carry the fight without a replacement. Another attempt at improvement was in the Model 52C which concentrated on increased firepower, more fuel tank protection and an over-all performance increase. Operational pilots felt that this would return the Zero's qualitative superiority it had lost to the Grumman F6F Hellcat. Designers knew, however, that they would severely overload their 1938-designed airframe in trying to assume 1944 standards. There were no options but to try.

The Navy issued a top priority order on 23 July, 1944, which called for a number of equipment changes and additions. Armament was again increased by adding two Type 3 13-mm wing mounted machine-guns outboard of the two 20-mm cannon. To adjust for some of this weight increase, the newly installed 13-mm nose machine-gun was eliminated altogether. Armament now consisted of five guns.

Adding to this firepower were the addition for the first time of underwing racks to accommodate small air-to-air rocket bombs.

Recognizing that the Zero was now far too often in front of the foe, armour plate was installed for the first time behind the pilot's seat and several panels of bullet resistant glass were added within the rear canopy.

To compensate for the loss in operational range that had occurred over previous modifications with the addition of weight, a 37-gallon self-sealing fuel tank was installed behind the pilot seat. All these modifications added up to more than 300 kg (660 lbs) over that of the previous model.

By now, the Zero's designer, Jiro Horikoshi, had moved on to the urgent project of designing the A7M *Reppu*, Allied code name "Sam," as Mitsubishi's replacement for the Zero. The task of these late modifications to the Zero were left to designer engineer Eitaro Sano. He could readily see that, with this vast increase in weight, the performance of the A6M5c would be greatly impaired if the *Sakae* 21 engine was to be retained. His team's proposal to the Naval Bureau of Aeronautics was to incorporate Mitsubishi's own engine of greater horsepower into the Zero. This new engine was the 1,350 hp *Kinsei* 62, which would provide an increase of 250 hp. With this engine, the design staff felt that the Zero might well be restored to a performance equal to that of the American F6F Hellcat.

To the grave disappointment of the designers, the Navy refused to release any of the larger engines, for most were already committed as an emergency replacement engine for the troublesome Aichi-built *Atsuta* in-line water-cooled engine used on the carrier dive bomber D4Y ("Judy") which was urgently needed in combat. Besides, the Navy claimed that the engineering time required for adapting this engine to the Zero airframe was prohibitive. As an alternate measure, the Navy recommended water-methanol injection be used with the *Sakae* engine for emergency power when needed. Mitsubishi's engineers were left with no choice, but this engine modification, now called the *Sakae* 31a, was slow in coming and the project had to continue with the existing series of the *Sakae* 21.

Nevertheless, the airframe modifications that were planned for, did continue. When the first A6M5c was completed in September 1944, the flight tests were disappointing, but were expected under the circumstances. The added weight without increase in power reduced performance considerably. Production was interrupted with this model when the new A6M6c showed promise, but with its failing, A6M5c production was resumed until 93 of this series was completed by the end of 1944.

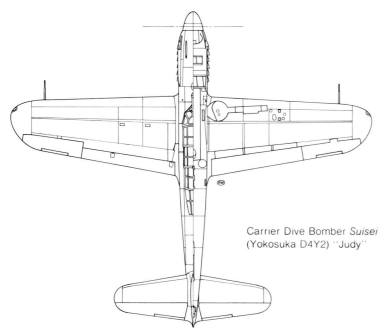

Carrier Dive Bomber *Suisei*
(Yokosuka D4Y2) "Judy"

Zero Model 53c, A6M6c

By November of that year, the water-methanol *Sakae* Model 31a was installed in a Zero airframe. Engineers also felt that self-sealing tanks were developed sufficiently for operational use and incorporated them for the first time in a Japanese aircraft. What was hoped to be a smooth transition on the existing A6M5c Model 52c assembly line to this new model, produced one more of many disappointments. The new engine failed to perform as expected. Not only was this engine reduced in power due to the modification, but the value on the new water-methanol metering system failed repeatedly during engine functional tests. A solution to the problem did not seem forthcoming. This uncertainty slowed production until the plan for using the modified engine and the equally troublesome self-sealing tanks was abandoned and production was resumed with the preceding Model 52c. Mitsubishi produced only one Zero 53c. Although its designation followed the prescribed pattern for airframe and engine model changes, the reason for the use of the suffix "c" in this case remains unclear.

Zero Model 63, A6M7:

The requirements for war continued to move ahead at a rate faster than Japan's aircraft industry could match. Deprived of its larger aircraft carriers by the fall of 1944, the Japanese Navy had difficulties in equipping its smaller carrier-borne units with suitable dive bombers. The Aichi D3A "Val" was far too slow and virtually defenseless against new Allied fighters. Its replacement, the Aichi D4Y3 "Judy" landed too fast to be safely operated from these carriers. A substitute had to be found in time to defend the Philippines against the coming Allied invasion.

Zeros were modified for the fighter-bomber mission which resulted in the Model 63. The armament remained the same as on the previous Model 52c, but a replacement of the normal 330 ltr (87 U.S. Gal) centre-line expendable auxiliary fuel tank, was a Mitsubishi-developed bomb rack capable of carrying a 250 kg (550 lb) bomb. Replacing the centre-line fuel tank were two wing-mounted 150 ltr (40 U.S. Gal) drop tanks, fitted outboard of the landing gear.

To compensate for added stresses encountered in the dive-bomber role, increased skin thickness was added to the tail of these models.

When this new model – many of which were modified from earlier types – was committed to combat in the Philippines, difficulty was often encountered with the bomb release mechanism. This frustration coupled with the desperate war situation for Japan led to some of the first recognized *kamikaze* attacks of the war by Zeros that carried their bomb loads directly into their targets.

Although existing records do not show a change back to the *Sakae* 21 engine for this model, some measure of success must have been achieved in the water-methanol modified engines. In addition to the "3" being retained instead of changing the designation to Zero Model 62, the one known example of a Model 63, which is in the collection of the U.S. National Air and Space Museum in Washington, is fitted with a *Sakae* 31b engine. Mitsubishi produced an undetermined

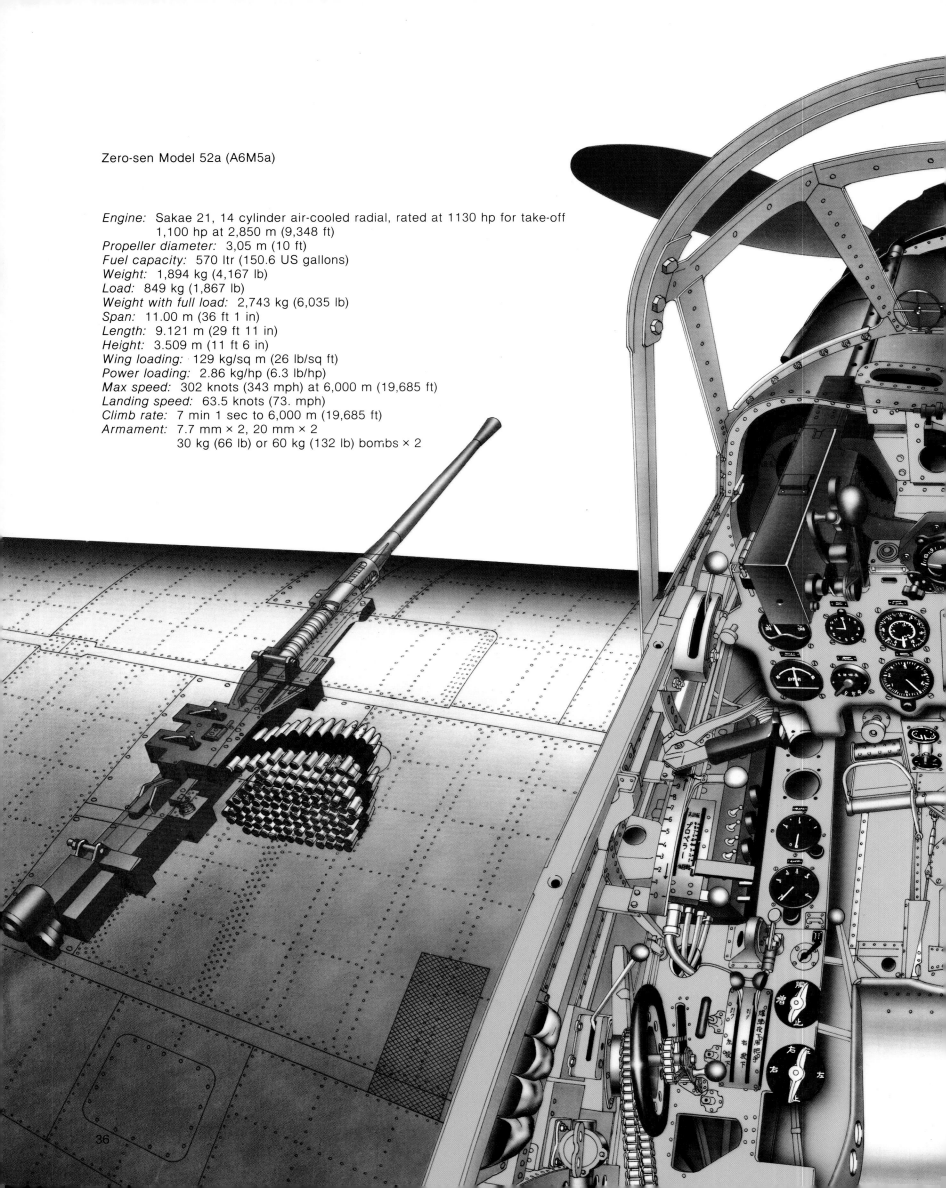

Zero-sen Model 52a (A6M5a)

Engine: Sakae 21, 14 cylinder air-cooled radial, rated at 1130 hp for take-off
          1,100 hp at 2,850 m (9,348 ft)
Propeller diameter: 3,05 m (10 ft)
Fuel capacity: 570 ltr (150.6 US gallons)
Weight: 1,894 kg (4,167 lb)
Load: 849 kg (1,867 lb)
Weight with full load: 2,743 kg (6,035 lb)
Span: 11.00 m (36 ft 1 in)
Length: 9.121 m (29 ft 11 in)
Height: 3.509 m (11 ft 6 in)
Wing loading: 129 kg/sq m (26 lb/sq ft)
Power loading: 2.86 kg/hp (6.3 lb/hp)
Max speed: 302 knots (343 mph) at 6,000 m (19,685 ft)
Landing speed: 63.5 knots (73. mph)
Climb rate: 7 min 1 sec to 6,000 m (19,685 ft)
Armament: 7.7 mm × 2, 20 mm × 2
               30 kg (66 lb) or 60 kg (132 lb) bombs × 2

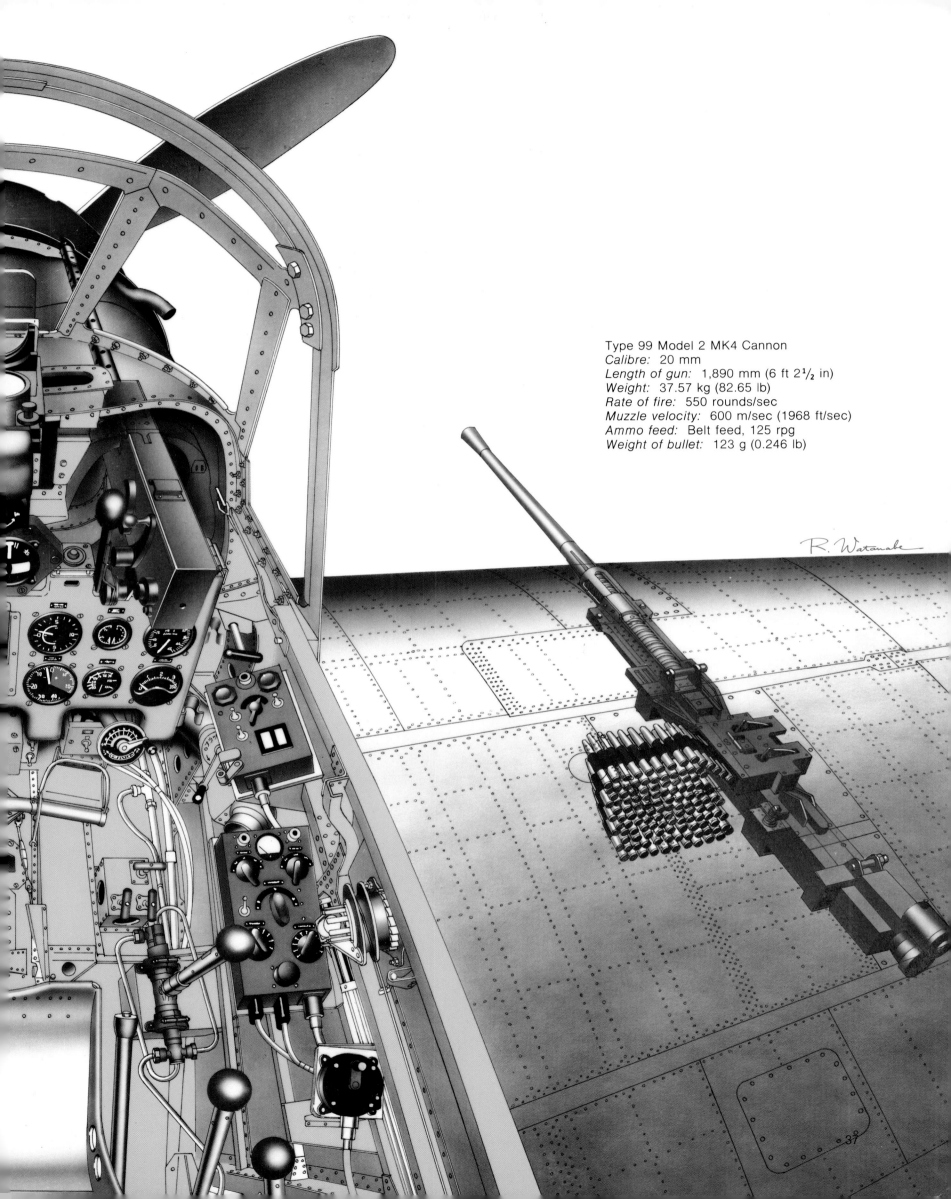

Type 99 Model 2 MK4 Cannon
Calibre: 20 mm
Length of gun: 1,890 mm (6 ft 2$\frac{1}{2}$ in)
Weight: 37.57 kg (82.65 lb)
Rate of fire: 550 rounds/sec
Muzzle velocity: 600 m/sec (1968 ft/sec)
Ammo feed: Belt feed, 125 rpg
Weight of bullet: 123 g (0.246 lb)

R. Watanabe

number of these models, starting their manufacture in May, 1945. Zeros within this group included Model 62, with the *Sakae* 21 engine, for some Allied Intelligence reports mention such a model designation along with Model 63.

Zero Model 54c, A6M8c:

Despite the resistance of the Japanese Navy to place a more powerful engine in the Zero airframe, a number of events finally reversed this decision. Not only had the aircraft continued to gain structural weight with each modification, but little or no added power was ever introduced to compensate. In addition, the clean lines of the fighter were being interrupted with bomb racks, drop tanks, more guns, and some external strengthening of the skin, all of which detracted from performance. Quality in production of both airframe and engines lessened as the war persisted with unskilled and drafted labour, and the relentless B-29 bombing raids. The Zero fighter may have retained the appearance of the earlier "hunter" when it first ruled the Pacific in the

opening months of the war, but now it was the "hunted," manned with under-trained pilots and having to cope with superior Allied fighters and better trained crews.

To follow the plan of replacing the Zero with Mitsubishi's new fighter the A7M1 *Reppu*, "Sam," production of the *Sakae* engine began tapering off to increase production of the new and more powerful *Homare* engine. Problems with the new aircraft necessitated continual production of the Zero but the supply of *Sakae* engines became critical. As a result, in November, 1944, the Navy agreed to install the Mitsubishi *Kinsei* 62 engine in newly produced Zero fighters. This had been Horikoshi's preference from a very early stage of development but its reality came too late, for now it was only a matter of time as the air war was all but lost.

Among other changes included in the new model were the elimination of the troublesome self-sealing fuel tanks, replacing their protection with a fire extinguishing system. Also included was an increase in fuel capacity for the thirstier engine in order to retain a flight time of 30 minutes at

1 Type 99 MK4 20mm cannon
2 20mm ammunition belt (125 rpg)
3 Gadget pocket
4 Emergency float blower lever
5 Machine-gun lock lever
6 Elevator trimming tab control
7 Rudder trimming tab control
8 Bomb release lever
9 Auxiliary fuel tank jettison lever
10 Wing tanks selector lever
11 Fuselage/wing-tanks switching cock
12 Wing tanks fuel gauge switching cock
13 Emergency fuel jettison lever
14 Wing tanks fuel gauge
15 Fuselage tank fuel gauge
16 Circuit breakers
17 Supercharger control
18 Propeller pitch control lever
19 Mixture control lever
20 Throttle lever
21 20mm cannon firing lever
22 High altitude automatic mixture control
23 Emergency power boost
24 Radio direction indicator

25 Magneto switch
26 Altimeter
27 Magnetic compass
28 Manifold pressure gauge
29 Oil temperature gauge
30 Cylinder head temperature gauge
31 Tachometer
32 Fuel & oil pressure gauge
33 Rate of climb indicator
34 Airspeed indicator
35 Clock
36 Exhaust temperature gauge
37 Artificial horizon
38 Turn & bank indicator
39 7.7mm type 97 machine-gun

40 Type 98 reflector gunsight
41 Inertia starter lever
42 Cowl flap control
43 Direction finder control unit
44 Fresh air duct
45 Radio control unit
46 Arresting hook winding wheel
47 Loop antenna handle
48 Flap control
49 Landing gear lever
50 Emergency fuel pump lever
51 Emergency gear-down lever
52 Wing tanks cooling air intake control
53 Oil cooler shutter control
54 Ignition booster switch
55 20mm cannon master switch
56 Oxygen supply gauge
57 Hydraulic pressure gauge
58 Primer
59 Foot pedal
60 Foot pedal position adjuster
61 Control column
62 Seat
63 Seat up/down lever

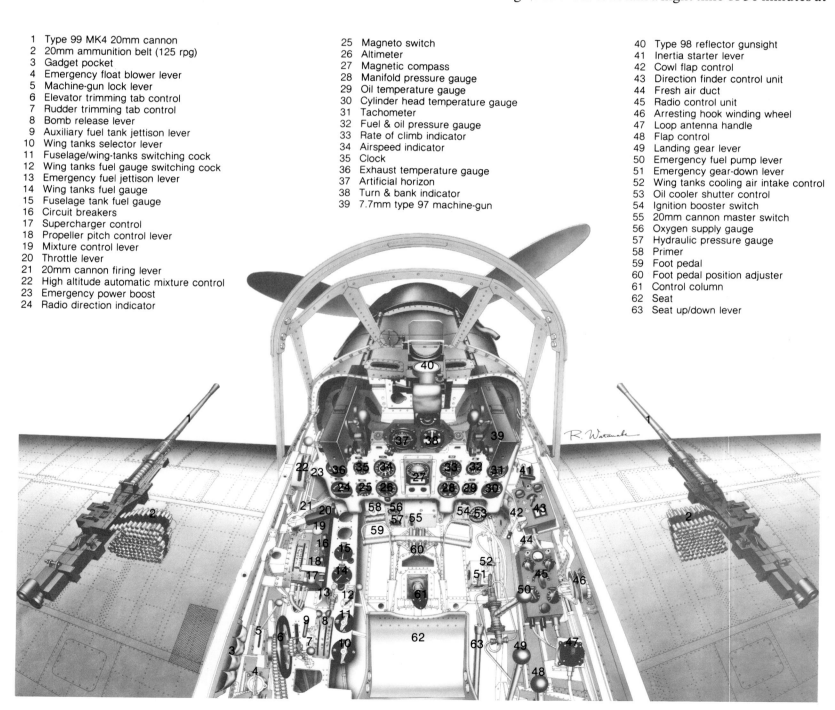

combat power, plus 2½ hours at normal cruise. The new engine increased the size of the nose appreciably, and with this added weight, the single nose-mounted Type 3, 13-mm machine-gun was eliminated.

By the end of March, 1945, the first prototype of the new series was expected to be completed, but extensive air-raid damage to the Mitsubishi dispersal plants had drastically delayed production. The effort for delivering the new machine was pressed home by Engineers Eitaro Sano, Kazuaki Izumi and Shiro Kushibe, and the first machine was flown in late April. The continuing war effort was taking its toll on everything being produced, and the new engine suffered from such things as low oil pressure, high oil temperature, and fluctuations in fuel pressure at various altitudes. Changes were made to correct these faults until finally the new aircraft achieved the expectations of Mitsubishi and the demands of the Navy.

The Navy accepted the first prototype of the A6M8c on 25 May, 1945, and one month later took delivery of the second. Maximum level-flight speed was recorded at 308 kts (355 mph) at 6,000 m (19,700 ft) along with the ability to climb to that altitude in 6 min 50 secs. Although this maximum level speed was 48 kts (55 mph) slower than the F4U-1D at that altitude, it showed a halt in the trend toward deteriorating performance which had prevailed since the spring or summer of 1944 in all Japanese aircraft. Test pilots who flew the Model 54c overwhelmingly agreed that this was the best model of the Zero yet produced.

Type 2 Fighter Seaplane, A6M2-N:

Before departing from these accounts in the development of the Zero, there was another model of this fighter that deserves mention in addition to two-seat trainer versions. This is the seaplane version of the Zero that the Allies code named "Rufe." In late 1940, Nakajima was already in production of the A6M2 when the Japanese Navy issued the 15-*Shi* specification calling for a single-seat seaplane fighter pending the development and production of the Kawanishi N1K1 *Kyofu*, known as "Rex." Its purpose was to provide air cover during the early phases of amphibious landing operations or over military bases of the small islands where the construction of airfields was not practical. As an interim aircraft, the Navy instructed Nakajima to develop a float fighter version of the Zero using the aircraft of the Model 11 without folding wing tips. The design modification that followed had the main float supported by a unique triangular type strut, and the wing tip float at both sides was attached by one slender strut. This float system ensured the least amount of drag, yet was sturdy enough for practical seaplane use.

A total of 327 "Rufe" fighters was manufactured early in the war, making them the first seaplane fighters to actually engage in combat. "Rufes" were active in the Aleutian Operation and in the Solomons. Despite the weight and drag of the floats, these fighters were fast and manoeuvrable. They served their mission very well initially, but in a short time they were unable to effectively counter Allied land-based fighters.

Type 2 Float Plane Fighter Model 11 (Nakajima A6M2-N) "Rufe"

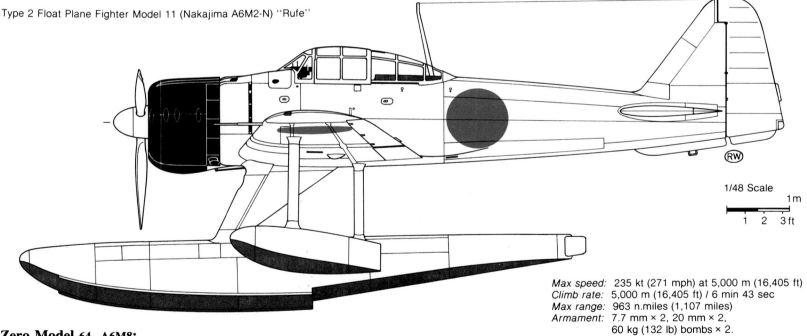

1/48 Scale

1m

1 2 3 ft

Max speed: 235 kt (271 mph) at 5,000 m (16,405 ft)
Climb rate: 5,000 m (16,405 ft) / 6 min 43 sec
Max range: 963 n.miles (1,107 miles)
Armament: 7.7 mm × 2, 20 mm × 2,
60 kg (132 lb) bombs × 2.

Zero Model 64, A6M8:

With this model, the final development of the Zero went into production with an overly optimistic order of 6,300 machines. Satisfied with the promising results demonstrated with the 1,350 hp *Kinsei* 62 powered Model 54, this Model 64 would have the fighter-bomber airframe of the earlier Model 63. Six major aircraft plants of both Mitsubishi and Nakajima were pressed into continued production of the Zero. But Japan failed to see another of the improved models come from their production lines, for time had run out and the surrender of Japan ended production.

Combat Rages On

First Allied experience with the Zero fighter was during missions for which it was designed. For the attack on Pearl Harbor, aircraft carriers of the Japanese fleet delivered the Zeros and bombers used in this attack within 200 nautical miles of the target. From that moment on the name "Zero Fighter" would never be forgotten.

The Zeros next appeared over Wake Island, destroying all opposing aircraft and gaining their superiority so that the invasion of that island was successful. From there, the Japanese military strength pushed further south in a string of victories, eventually attacking Port Darwin, Australia, by mid-February, 1942. Zero fighters provided air cover for each of these operations during which air superiority was maintained throughout. For this campaign, instead of operating from aircraft carriers as the Allies were again certain was

The day following this attack, Clark Air Base in the Philippines was left in burning rubble by Japanese bombers escorted by Zeros of the Tainan *Kokutai* (Air Corps). The Americans were convinced that the fighters had been launched from nearby aircraft carriers, which is the way the plan was first intended. Instead, after confirming the long range capabilities of the Zero, these strikes at targets in the Philippines originated and terminated from bases on Formosa, a round trip distance of 900 nautical miles (nearly 1,125 statute miles) leaving sufficient time for combat engagements in the target area. The long range designed into the Zero was put to the ultimate test, which freed the otherwise needed aircraft carriers for other strikes. By 13 December, after five days of attack, the U.S. air forces had been virtually annihilated throughout the Philippines.

the case, they did in reality fly from newly captured land bases on Timor Island, 400 nautical miles (460 statute miles) to the northwest. The Allies could not fully grasp the true capabilities of the Zero to cover such distances and then function so well as a fighter.

The tide of the Japanese military power went unchecked over the vast area of the Pacific and its many islands until the great naval engagement in the Coral Sea on 7 and 8 May, 1942. This was the first battle engagement ever to be fought entirely by aircraft with the surface ships out of sight of each other. During the two-day battle, the A6M2s fought ruthlessly in this first real challenge to Japanese air superiority. This situation was not a matter of superiority of one fighter against another, but one fighter force against another fighter force. The Zero was challenged by the chunky

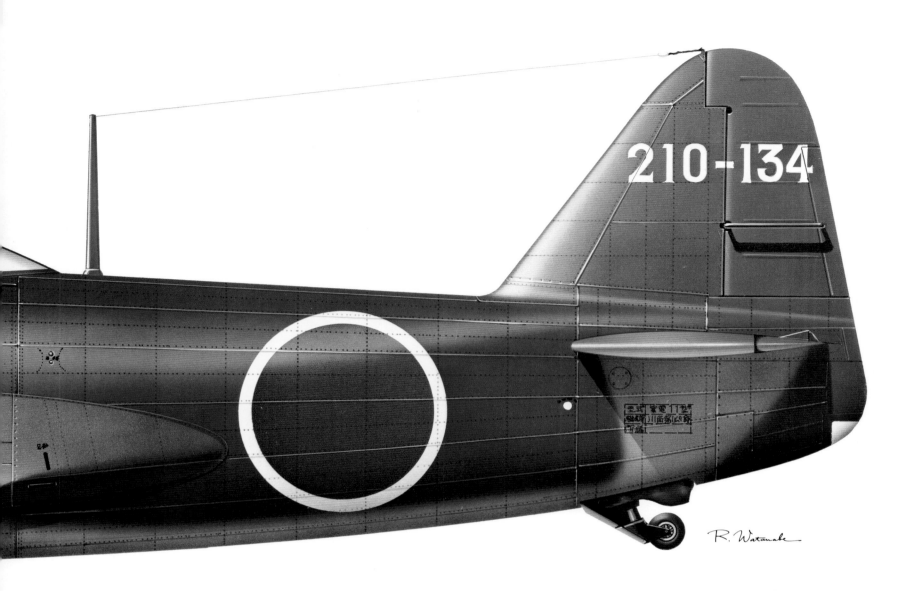

Kawanishi N1K1-J *Shiden*

Delays with the *Raiden* fighter ('Jack') prompted the Japanese Navy to look into other possibilities for an air superiority fighter. In March, 1944, the decision was made to redirect priorities from that of the ailing *Raiden* to the Kawanishi N1K1-J *Shiden*, better known as 'George,' while continuing with the production of the Zero fighter. At first, the Navy was reluctant to fully recognize the potential of the *Shiden* since Kawanishi made it a private venture to convert their *Kyofu* N1K1 seaplane fighter design 'Rex' into a land-based fighter.

This conversion had its own share of technical problems. Utilizing the 1,990 hp Homare engine which was over 500 hp more than the seaplane version, its resultant large propeller required a long landing gear

from its mid-wing configuration for sufficient ground clearance. From the start of flight testing in December, 1942, its progress was marred by problems. Like so many of the unproven engines, the Homare failed to develop its rated power. The long landing gear legs which contracted as they retracted into the wheel wells often failed.

Many of the airframe design problems were resolved by a new version of 'George,' designated N1K2-J. With a redesigned fuselage to simplify manufacture, the wing was relocated to the bottom of the fuselage, thus allowing for a shorter and more reliable landing gear retracting arrangement.

In combat, 'George' was regarded as an ineffictive interceptor due to its relatively poor climbing capability. However, the *Shiden Kai*, as it was named, was considered an outstanding fighter in air engagements on equal terms with the best Allied fighter aircraft.

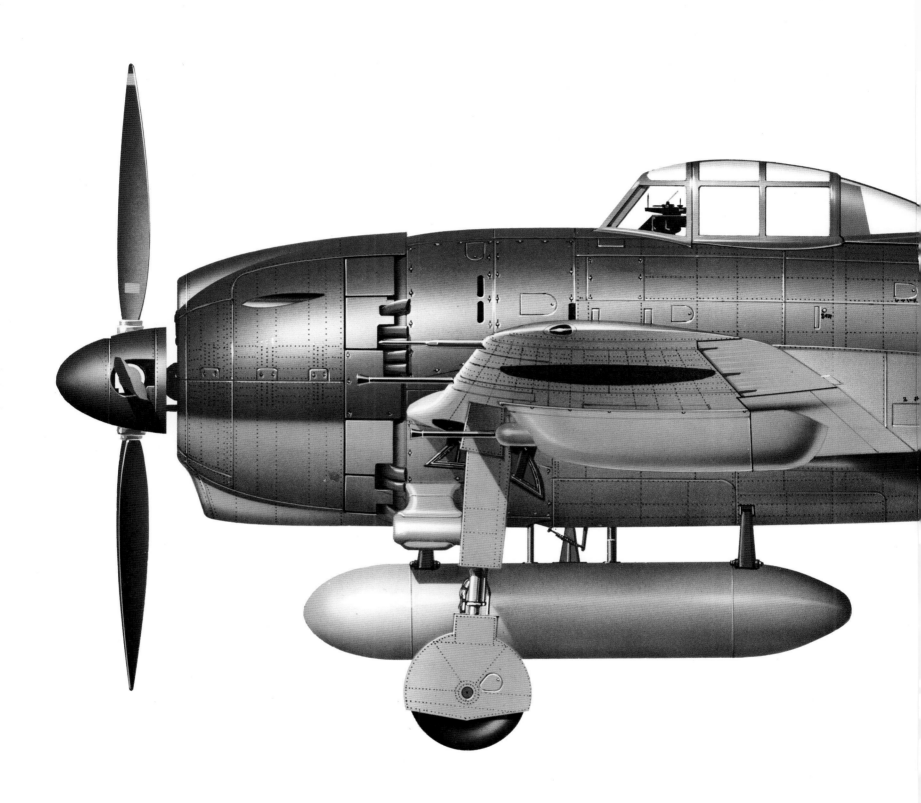

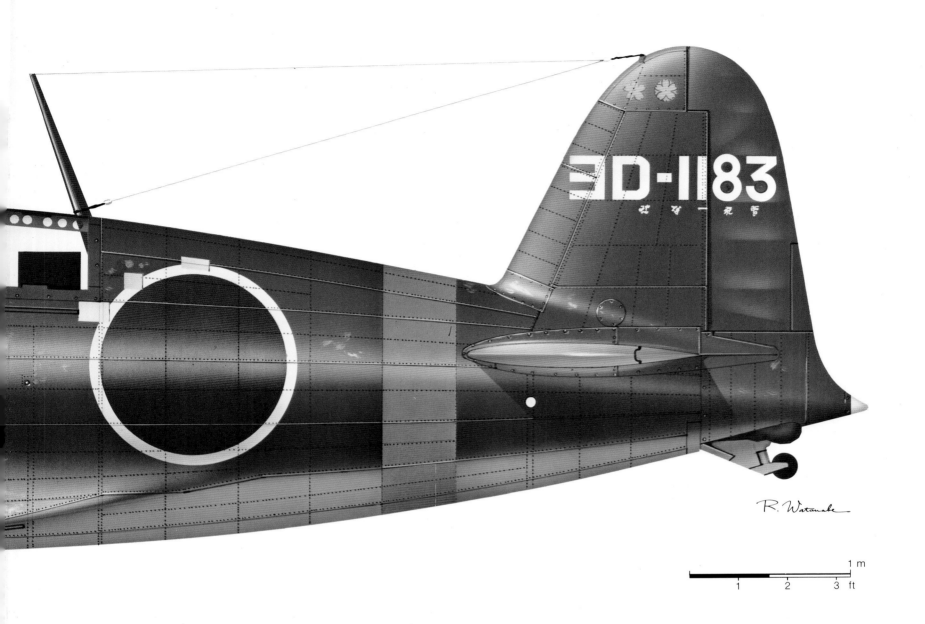

R. Watanabe

1 m

1   2   3 ft

Mitsubishi J2M3 *Raiden*

'Jack,' as the Allies code named the Mitsubishi J2M *Raiden*, was the Japanese Navy's first purely air defense interceptor. Conceived as the 14-*Shi* Interceptor Fighter in 1939, after proposal for the Zero had been established, the *Raiden* was intended to augment, not replace the Zero. As the war progressed, however, and the air war for Japan became that of defense, there was a greater need for this type aircraft than first envisioned.

The design concept of the *Raiden* centered around a snuggly cowled 1,800 hp Kasei radial engine, aircooled by a fan at the front. An extended drive shaft placed the propeller well forward of the engine which allowed the shape of the nose to be slender and give a more aerodynamic teardrop shape to the fuselage. The wings incorporated the newly developed laminar airflow section.

Problems with the engine and related vibration delayed its acceptance by the Navy as a service airplane until October, 1942. The first production airplane was not delivered until December, 1943. Preoccupation by Mitsubishi in the manufacture of the Zero contributed to some of this delay in solving technical problems and accelerating production. Finally, in despair, the Navy transferred the production of *Raiden* to a satellite plant of Mitsubishi, while the main Nagoya plant concentrated on the Zero. In all of several models, about 470 *Raidens* were built. Although it still retained the undesirable features of poor visibility, engine vibration, and short flight duration, its outstanding speed and climb made 'Jack' the most successful fighter used against the B-29 Superfortress.

Kyushu J7W1 *Shinden*

A prime example of Japanese aircraft design ingenuity after the development of the Zero was the *canard*-type Kyushu J7W1 *Shinden* fighter. Having the appearance of a futuristic fighter for the World War II time-period, it was the only tail-first design of several throughout the world that was regarded as a production aircraft. Plans were laid for mass production even before the first prototype was completed.

Unaware of experiments conducted in other countries with fighters of the *canard* type, a design team at the Yokosuka Air Technical Arsenal conceived a short-range intercepter early in 1943 which embodied this configuration. None of the existing interceptor programs in Japan were attaining success and the state of the art was surpassing their design before any of these fighters could be produced. The

Shinden was to be of advanced technology in hopes of closing this gap.

Much of the design work for the J7W1 was carried out at the Air Arsenal which included a series of tests with gliders and powered craft of the *canard* configuration. Results were so successful that the Navy ordered the *Shinden* into immediate production. The project for this unorthodox fighter was passed to the Kyushu Airplane Company since they were the only major airframe manufacturer not already committed to a priority fighter production. Navy engineers were so confident of the potentialities of this fighter that their chief designer, Lt. Cmdr. M. Tsuruno was sent to Kyushu to supervise development until production status was attained. The *Shinden* was an all metal airplane with a 2,000 hp Mitsubishi Ha 43-42 eighteen cylinder air-cooled radial engine mounted in the rear, driving a 6-blade propeller. The front-mounted horizontal surface acted as an elevator for flight

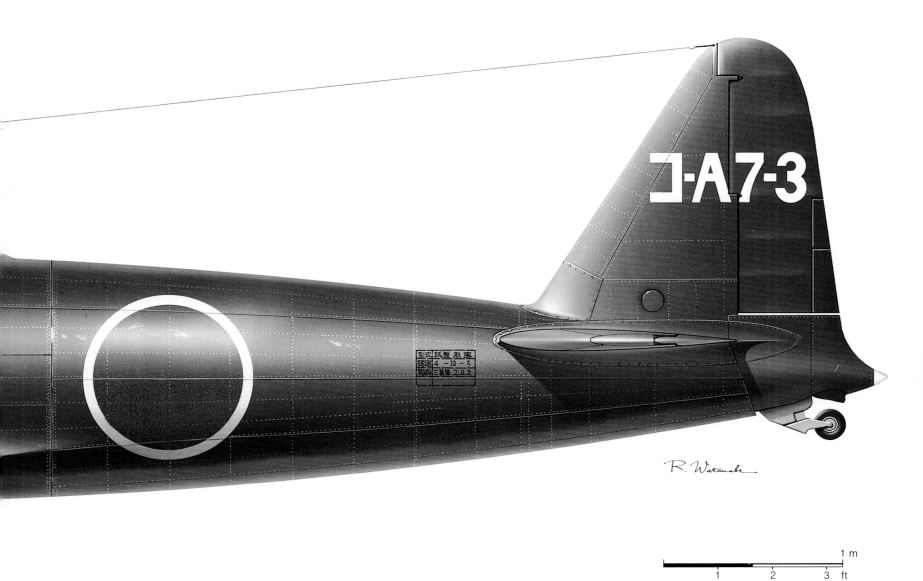

R. Watanabe

1 m

1   2   3 ft

Mitsubishi A7M2 *Reppu*

Had the Japanese Navy's plan succeeded for producing the Mitsubishi A7M *Reppu*, code-named 'Sam,' it could well have restored the air superiority Japan enjoyed in the first year of the war. Initially designed to be powered by a Mitsubishi 2,200 hp Ha 43 engine, the plane's size was comparable to the Republic P-47N Thunderbolt, yet the P-47s empty weight was 1.6 times greater than 'Sam.' With combat flaps, 'Sam's' maneuverability was said to have equaled that of the Zero fighter.

Conceived as early as April, 1942, when Mitsubishi was instructed to begin the design of the *Reppu* carrier-borne fighter to the 17-*Shi* specifications, it met with nothing but indecisions on the part of the Japanese Navy. After months of delays, the Navy finally insisted on a lesser-powered engine than the design had intended for meeting per-

formance requirements. Redesigning the airframe to carry the smaller engine further delayed completing the test airplane. This lack of sufficient power proved itself during the initial flight tests in May, 1944. Despite this handicap, 'Sam' demonstrated the handling qualities of being a formidable opponent against Allied fighters.

The Navy now reversed its decision and approved the originally intended engine. With reengineering needed once again, the new A7M2, was finally flight tested in October, 1944. Having achieved the expected performance, the Navy ordered *Reppu* into production. By now serious material shortages, Allied bombing attacks, and the destructive earthquake of December, 1944, prevented more than the eight prototype aircraft from being completed. After more than three years in the development program, not one combat capable *Reppu* was produced—an airplane intended to replace the ageing and outclassed Zero fighter which had to see the war through to the last day.

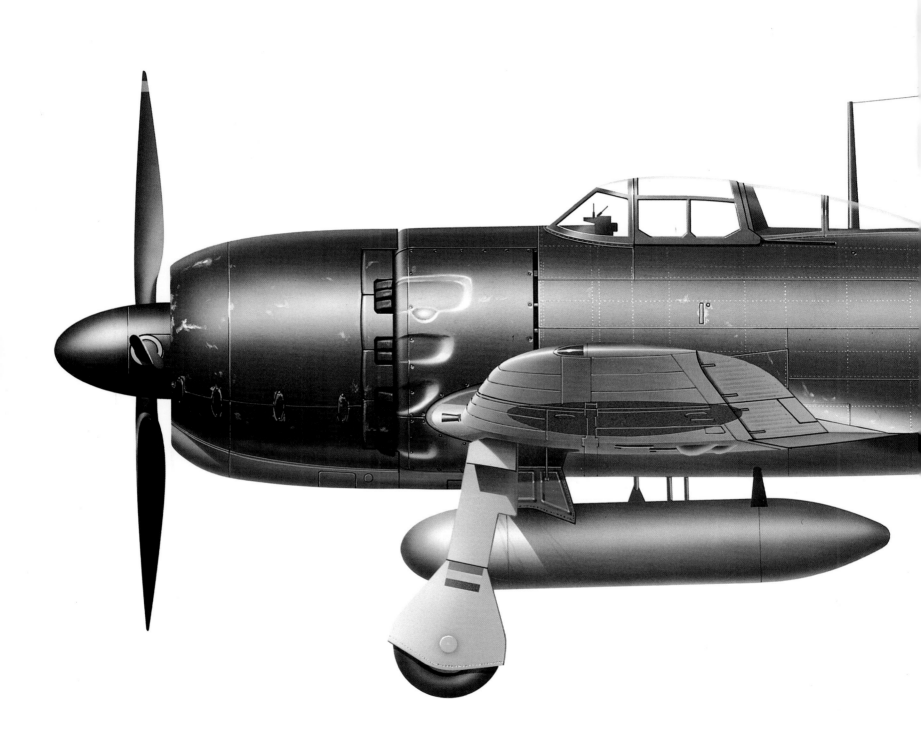

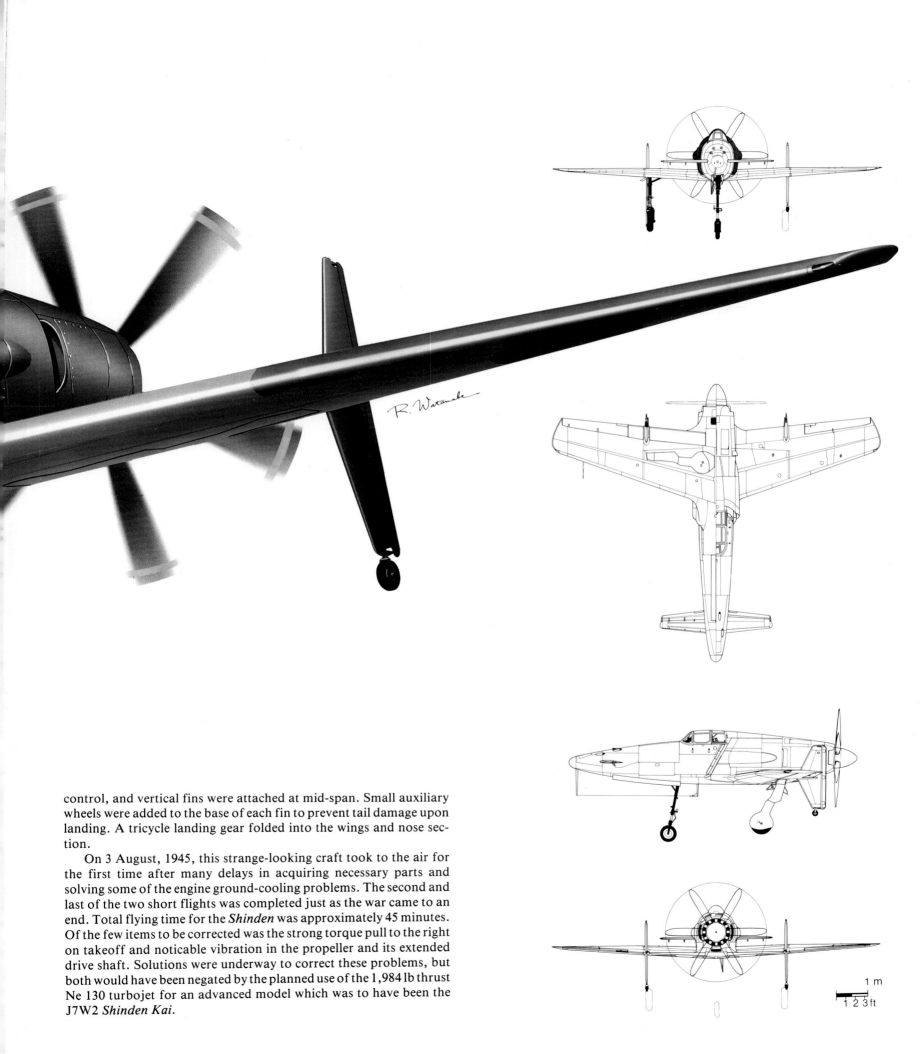

R. Watanabe

control, and vertical fins were attached at mid-span. Small auxiliary wheels were added to the base of each fin to prevent tail damage upon landing. A tricycle landing gear folded into the wings and nose section.

On 3 August, 1945, this strange-looking craft took to the air for the first time after many delays in acquiring necessary parts and solving some of the engine ground-cooling problems. The second and last of the two short flights was completed just as the war came to an end. Total flying time for the *Shinden* was approximately 45 minutes. Of the few items to be corrected was the strong torque pull to the right on takeoff and noticable vibration in the propeller and its extended drive shaft. Solutions were underway to correct these problems, but both would have been negated by the planned use of the 1,984 lb thrust Ne 130 turbojet for an advanced model which was to have been the J7W2 *Shinden Kai*.

1 m

1 2 3 ft

Grumman F4F of near equal power, but the Japanese fighter with its lighter weight gave it the advantage of manoeuvrability, speed, rate of climb and acceleration – everything that was planned in its design. The ability of the Wildcat to absorb punishment was without a doubt its redeeming feature, but this did not give the American pilots any great advantage where flight performance was generally the deciding factor. Fighter team tactics by the U.S. Navy pilots had much to do with shifting the advantage to the Wildcat.

longer dominated the ocean. Thus ended the Zero's operations from the heavy carriers of the Japanese fleet, and the only thing Japan had accomplished during this battle was the seizing of the tiny, uninhabited islands of Attu and Kiska in the Aleutians as a diversionary effort of the major battle at Midway. This gain was perhaps countered, for it was from this northern operation that the Americans were able to gain a downed Zero and discover, for the first time, its innermost secrets.

◄ Admiral Yamamoto, Commander-in-Chief of the Japanese Combined Fleet, watching a *Zero 21* taking off from Rabaul. He died on 18 April, 1943, while on his way to Buin Airbase, about ten days after this picture was taken.

▼ *Zero 22s* of the First Naval Air Corps in Rabaul engaging in Operation *Ro-Go*. The operation (November 2-12, 1943), involving 80 pilots and 82 Zeros, ended with a loss of 24 pilots and 43 planes.

By June, 1942, the Japanese fleet, supported by carrier-based Zeros, attempted to invade Midway Island. The element of surprise was thought by the Japanese to be on their side, but the Americans were prepared for the attack. The battle started favourably for the Japanese when they successfully defended their carriers against attack and the American forces took heavy aerial losses. As the battle progressed and the attention of the Japanese was switched to the low flying U.S. torpedo bombers attacking their ships, U.S. dive bombers came in steeply overhead and unloaded their 1,000 pound bombs, many of them squarely on the Japanese carriers. Three were sunk and a fourth set on fire. With them went 234 Japanese aircraft. This became the turning point of the Pacific War. With these losses of principal ships and the fighter cover provided by the Zero, Japanese warships no

With Japan's shortage of aircraft carriers, the heavy arresting gear hooks were removed from a number of Zeros as air units were assigned to land base operations only. During the late spring and early summer of 1942, the only major Japanese Navy air action against the Allies came from the 25th Air Flotilla, headquartered at Rabaul. Aircraft from this air unit engaged in constant air attacks, concentrated against Allied installations at Port Moresby in New Guinea. Lesser attacks were directed at such places as Port Darwin and Timor, to prevent the Allies from concentrating all their defences on centralized points. Japanese medium bombers were escorted by a comparative number of Zero fighters on these sorties.

To support the ultimate plan for taking Port Moresby, the Japanese attacked Buna in mid-July, 1942, on the north-east coast of New Guinea. This erupted in fierce fighting as each side tried to counter their enemy's next move. When the Allies launched their invasion of Guadalcanal in the southern group of the Solomon Islands, this was the first attempt by the Americans to strike back at the Japanese. This combined air, land and sea assault by the Allies started the long road to recovering lost ground.

In this early phase of fighting, the Zero fighters operating from Salumaua and Lae, put up what was unquestionably the toughest fighter opposition Allied pilots experienced throughout the Pacific war. At these advanced bases were Japan's greatest aces of the Imperial Navy. The Zero was still superior to the P-39s and P-40s as well as the Wildcats they were encountering, but the American pilots were gaining in skill and tactics which were able to defeat the Zero. The long period of repeated victories for the Japanese was nearing the end as the year 1942 came to a close.

An assortment of superior American fighters was beginning to be introduced to the Pacific conflict in late 1942 at the same time the Japanese had programmed for their replacement of the Zero. Japan's new Navy fighters were slow to be developed and the Zero was left to hold the line as best it could. Starting in 1943, the most frequent opponent of the Zero was the Grumman Hellcat, a carrier-based fighter that could take on the Japanese opposition under any conditions. One reason was that its original pre-Pearl Harbor design had been specifically altered to combat the Zero, based on the lessons learned by U.S. Navy pilots in the early days of fighting. When the Lockheed P-38 Lightning and Vought F4U Corsair appeared on the scene, they were superior to the Zero in nearly every respect except manoeuvrability. Allied aircrews developed tactics of a type that countered the Japanese attempt to engage in dogfights which would give the Zero the advantage. Other fighters followed such as the Republic P-47 Thunderbolt, and much later, the North American P-51 Mustang. There were many air battles during the months that followed in which the Zero was often present. The most often recorded and discussed is the battle of the Philippine Sea. This battle erupted when the Japanese fleet attempted to counter the Allied invasion of the Marianas Islands.

The Japanese task force west of the islands, consisting of nine aircraft carriers and other major ships, had prepared for shuttle attacks against the American invading Task Force that was positioned between the Japanese fleet and the Japanese-held islands. Shortly after dawn on 19 June, 1944, the Japanese carriers began sending their planes on their strike mission against the American ships and landing assault forces. Having guessed the plan of the Japanese, the F6F Hellcats were already waiting high above the fleet. As the Japanese planes appeared, the American fighters dived down upon them in a devastating coordinated attack.

Over a period of eight hours, four successive waves of Japanese planes flew in from the southwest, in groups averaging about one hundred each. The same fate was experienced by each wave. Only about forty of the Japanese aircraft got through the defending fighters, and half of these were shot down by the ships' curtain of intense anti-aircraft fire.

About 370 Japanese planes were shot down during this spectacular aerial battle which history refers to as the "Marianas Turkey Shoot." Counting the land-based Japanese planes that took off for these islands earlier that morning and were shot down, total Japanese losses for the day were more than 400 aircraft. Of the original 450 Japanese planes used during the battle, only one in 10 had survived. On the remaining carriers not sunk that day, only six torpedo-bombers, two dive bombers, 12 attack-bombers, and a mere 25 of the original compliment of 225 Zero fighters remained. Twenty-six American planes were lost, and about half of their pilots were saved.

These results, of course, are very one-sided. The Zero fighter had not lessened in its performance or capability, in fact it had improved. Either because of Japanese tactical error, or because of the poor state of training of the Japanese pilots for an operation of this size, the attack came in widely separated and ill-coordinated waves. This allowed the American aircraft time to reservice and rearm. The Japanese pilots were also in a semi-exhausted state after flying nearly 350 nautical miles from their carriers, supposedly out of reach of U.S. planes, and were therefore at a disadvantage to evade the fierce and overwhelming attacks by the F6F Hellcats.

There was more to be blamed for these heavy losses than undertrained crews and outdated equipment. A trait found in most Japanese aircraft that were encountered early in the war was their inability to withstand enemy gunfire, and the Zero was no exception. Their lack of pilot protection devices, such as armour plate and fire-resisting self-sealing fuel tanks were items omitted from nearly all these early war period aircrafts, a concept based on recommendations made by seasoned combat pilots. They were more concerned in obtaining the best performance resulting from minimum weight for concentrating on *attack*, than the lack of safety features which to them represented encumbering luxury. It was not uncommon that pilots left their parachutes on the

(National Archives)

ground in order to reduce weight for an added advantage in any air duel.

The point must be stressed, however, that these design shortcomings from adequate protection were not an oversight by the designers. What was missing from the very beginning was a good 1,200 hp engine to carry the necessary safeguards for aircraft and pilot without sacrificing performance. As was the case with Allied planes, more power should have been added over the years as the Zero was improved with its inherent weight penalties. Horikoshi did extremly well with the limited horsepower that was available to him for the Zero.

As the Pacific war went on, and the Allies introduced new fighters possessing greater firepower and speed, the attitudes of Japanese pilots began to change as their losses continued to increase. Beginning with the Zero 52, modifications including pilot protective features and fire suppression devices originally scorned were being added at a sacrifice in performance. But the tide of battle had already turned against Japan and the previous lack of protective measures through much of the war had already cut deeply into their equipment and highly skilled pilots.

Model 52 and the Americans

The battle of the Marianas and the capture of Saipan in June, 1944, placed the improved Model 52 Zero into American hands for the first time. Allied airmen had been encountering the newer model as early as the previous fall, recognizing it primarily by a surprising increase in performance. Now they had their first chance for a closer look and flight evaluation of the improved Zero.

Twelve of these newly captured Zeros were sent from Saipan to the United States for study by the Technical Air Intelligence Centre. Several were rebuilt to be flown and

by the end of 1944, comparison flight tests had been made with various American fighters. The narrative report made of these findings has evaded publication over the years, though often sought by many historians. The intelligence summary gives comparative details recorded when the Zero was flown against the Vought F4U-1D Corsair, Grumman F6F-5 Hellcat and Eastern (Grumman) FM-2 Wildcat.

F4U-1D vs Zero 52:

Both aircrafts were flown side by side, making all things equal at the beginning of this flight comparison test. In a race for altitude, the best climb of the F4U-1D was equal to the Zero up to 10,000 ft, above 750 ft/min better at 18,000 feet and above 500 ft/min better at 22,000 feet and above. Best climb speeds of the F4U and Zero were 156 mph (135 kts) and 122 mph (105 kts) indicated air speed, respectively.

The F4U-1D was faster than the Zero 52 at all altitudes, having the least margin of 42 mph (37.5 kts) at 5,000 feet and the widest difference of 80 mph (70 kts) at 25,000 feet. Top speeds attained were 413 mph (360 kts) TAS at 20,400 feet for the Corsair and 335 mph (290 kts) TAS at 18,000 feet for the Zero.

Rate of roll for the Zero was equal to that of the Corsair at speeds under 230 mph (200 kts) and inferior above that speed due to the high control forces. Manoeuvrability of the Zero was remarkable at speeds below 202 mph (175 kts). being far superior to that of the Corsair. In slow speed turns the Zero could gain one turn in three and a half at 10,000 feet. At speeds around 202 mph (175 kts) however, the F4U could, by using flaps, stay with the Zero for about one-half turn, or until its speed fell off to 173 mph (150 kts).

Initial dive accelerations of the Zero and the Corsair were about the same after which the Corsair was far superior, and slightly superior in zooms after dives.

F6F vs Zero 52:

The Zero climbed about 600 ft/min better than the F6F up to 9,000 feet, after which the advantage fell off gradually until the two aircraft were about equal at 14,000 feet.

(National Archives)

51

Above this altitude the Hellcat had the advantage, varying from 500 ft/min better at 22,000 ft, to about 250 ft/min better at 30,000 feet. Best climb speeds of the F6F-5 and Zero 52 were 150 mph (130 kts) and 122 mph (105 kts) indicated, respectively.

The F6F-5 was faster than the Zero 52 at all altitudes, having the least margin of 25 mph (21.5 kts) at 5,000 feet and the widest difference of 75 mph (65 kts) at 25,000 feet. Top speeds attained were 409 mph (355 kts) at 21,600 feet for the Hellcat, and 335 mph (290 kts) at 18,000 feet for the Zero.

(Comments on rate of roll, dive, maneouvrability and turns for the Hellcat were identical to those made on the F4U except that attempts at turning with flaps was not mentioned.)

FM-2 vs Zero 52:

The FM-2 was a General Motors built Wildcat having a 1,350 hp engine replacing the 1,200 hp engine on the earlier F4F-4 previously described. In climbs, the Zero was about 400 ft/min less than that of the Wildcat starting at sea level, becoming equal at 4,000 feet and 400 ft/min better at 8,000 feet. Climbs became equal again passing 13,000 feet, and the Zero was only slightly inferior above 13,000 feet. Best climb speeds of the FM-2 and Zero were 138 mph (120 kts) and 122 mph (105 kts) indicated, respectively.

The FM-2 was 6 mph (5 kts) faster than the Zero at sea level becoming 4 mph (3.5 kts) slower at 5,000 feet and dropped to 26 mph (22.5 kts) slower at 30,000 feet. Top speeds attained were 321 mph (288 kts) TAS at 13,000 feet for the FM-2 and 335 mph (290 kts) at 18,000 feet for the Zero.   Rate of roll of the two fighters was equal at 184 mph (160 kts) and under. The Zero became inferior at higher speeds due to heavy stick forces. Turns of the FM-2 and Zero were very similar, with a slight advantage in favour of the Zero 52. The Zero could gain one turn in eight at 10,000 feet.

The Zero was slightly superior to the FM-2 in initial dive acceleration, after which the dives were about the same. Zooms after dives were about equal for the two aircraft.

Suggested Tactics: For engaging in combat with the Zero, all three American aircraft were not to dogfight with the Japanese fighter and not to follow it in a loop or half-roll with pull-through. When attacking, the superior power and speed performance of the F6F-5 and F4U-1D was to be used for engaging the Zero at the most favourable moment. For the FM-2, any altitude advantage possible was to be maintained. In all three cases, to evade a Zero, the best method was to roll and dive away in a high speed turn.

From this American report describing the performance of the later model Zero and how to cope with it, the point was obvious that the aircraft was still a serious threat in any air battle. The weakest aspect of the Zero fighter at this stage of its operational life was the lack of skilled pilots to fly them. It can be safely assumed that the American pilots flying the Zero for these tests were far more qualified through experience and training than the Japanese pilots normally encountered in combat.

Offspring of the Zero

The Imperial Japanese Navy had not expected the war to be prolonged as it was, nor for the service life of the Zero to be so extended. In addition to an array of Japanese Army fighters that opposed Allied air power, there were other Navy fighters, proposed or in being, to augment the Zero fighter. Technical production problems prevented these aircraft to do much to overshadow the dependency that the Navy placed upon the Zero.

Among these aircraft was Mitsubishi's J2M1 *Raiden*, code named "Jack" by the Allies. This was a radical change in Japanese single-seat fighter concepts in that for the first time, manoeuvrability became a secondary consideration to speed and climb. "Jack" was purely an interceptor intended to destroy enemy bombers as well as to out-perform enemy escort fighters. This concept from which evolved the 14-*Shi* fighter *Raiden*, began only two years after that of the Zero and before it had made its first flight.

By the time of the first test flight of the new aircraft on 20 March, 1942, Mitsubishi's production and technical skills were heavily committed to the Zero and other military aircraft that were in great demand. The project languished in development due primarily to problems with engine vibration and poor visibility for the pilot. These were not resolved until 1943, at which time limited production did get underway. Because of poor production management for an aircraft that was slowly to replace the Zero in the production lines, emphasis remained with the Zero and production of "Jack" was transferred to a subsidiary plant of Mitsubishi. In all, only 470 of the J2M1 interceptors were manufactured.

Meanwhile, as "Jack" was suffering with ever mounting technical problems, the Navy looked to Kawanishi with possibilities of converting their 15-*Shi Kyofu* seaplane fighter design into a land based interceptor. This design change became the N1K1-J *Shiden*, that the Allies code named "George". Due to its mid-wing that was suited for the seaplane design, and its huge propeller turned by a 1,990 hp Nakajima *Homare* 21 engine, the landing gear for the land based version had to be unusually long. This brought about numerous problems with strength and linkage that prompted the design to evolve into a low wing configuration in order to shorten the landing gear length.

In March, 1944, the Japanese Navy decided to replace the languishing production of "Jack" with the "George," while still continuing production with the proven Zero until it could adequately be replaced. In all 1,400 "George" interceptor fighters were produced in the mid-wing and low-wing versions.

All this while, the Japanese Navy was counting on Mitsubishi's A7M1 *Reppu* carrier-borne fighter, code named "Sam" as a replacement for the Zero. The A7M design was initiated in 1942 by Horikoshi to restore to Japan the air superiority it enjoyed in the brief first year of the war. With intentions of powering the new fighter with a 2,200 hp engine, there was every reason to believe that this new fighter would be superior to the American fighters it would one day oppose.

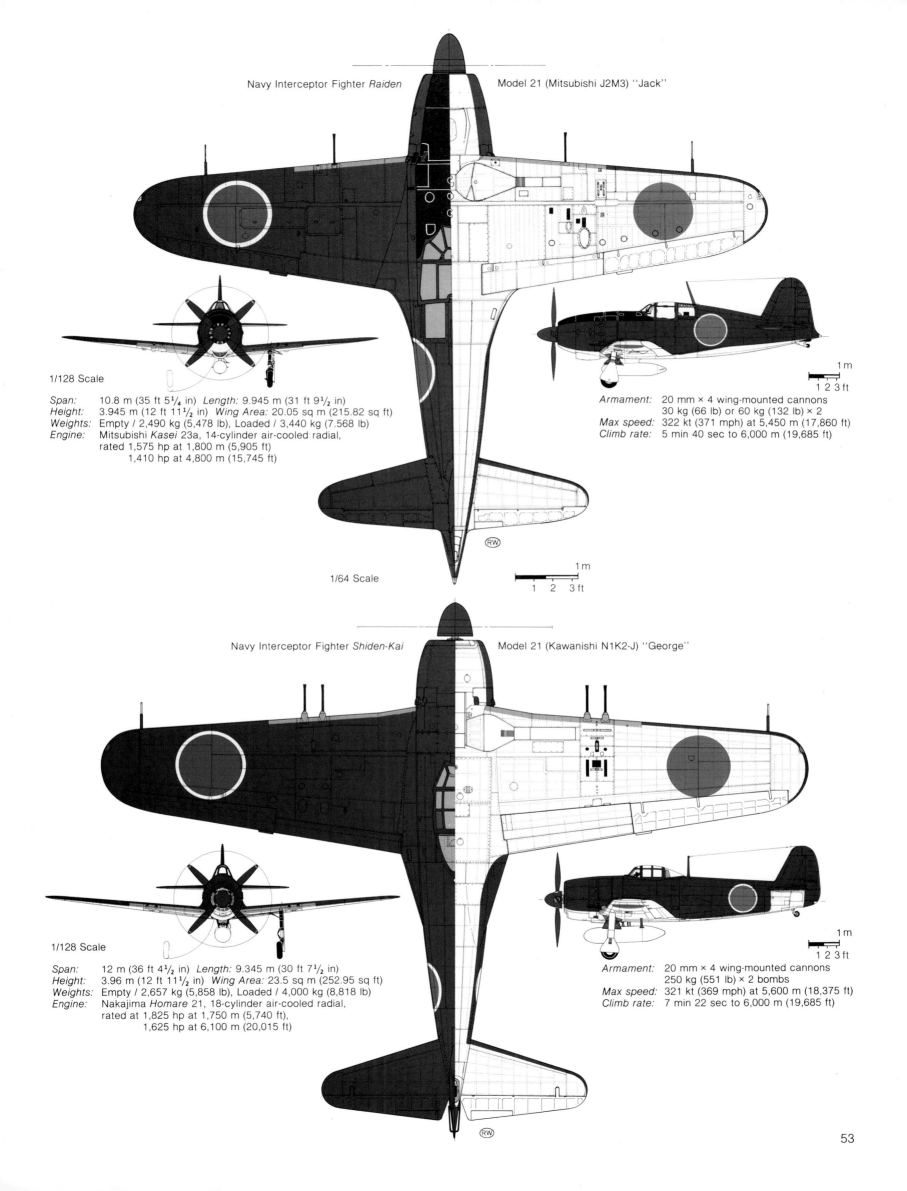

Navy Interceptor Fighter *Raiden*　　Model 21 (Mitsubishi J2M3) "Jack"

1/128 Scale

Span:　　10.8 m (35 ft 5¼ in)　*Length:* 9.945 m (31 ft 9½ in)
Height:　3.945 m (12 ft 11½ in)　*Wing Area:* 20.05 sq m (215.82 sq ft)
Weights: Empty / 2,490 kg (5,478 lb), Loaded / 3,440 kg (7.568 lb)
Engine:　Mitsubishi *Kasei* 23a, 14-cylinder air-cooled radial,
　　　　　rated 1,575 hp at 1,800 m (5,905 ft)
　　　　　1,410 hp at 4,800 m (15,745 ft)

Armament:　20 mm × 4 wing-mounted cannons
　　　　　　30 kg (66 lb) or 60 kg (132 lb) × 2
Max speed:　322 kt (371 mph) at 5,450 m (17,860 ft)
Climb rate:　5 min 40 sec to 6,000 m (19,685 ft)

1 m
1 2 3 ft

1/64 Scale

1 m
1 2 3 ft

Navy Interceptor Fighter *Shiden-Kai*　　Model 21 (Kawanishi N1K2-J) "George"

1/128 Scale

Span:　　12 m (36 ft 4½ in)　*Length:* 9.345 m (30 ft 7½ in)
Height:　3.96 m (12 ft 11½ in)　*Wing Area:* 23.5 sq m (252.95 sq ft)
Weights: Empty / 2,657 kg (5,858 lb), Loaded / 4,000 kg (8,818 lb)
Engine:　Nakajima *Homare* 21, 18-cylinder air-cooled radial,
　　　　　rated at 1,825 hp at 1,750 m (5,740 ft),
　　　　　1,625 hp at 6,100 m (20,015 ft)

Armament:　20 mm × 4 wing-mounted cannons
　　　　　　250 kg (551 lb) × 2 bombs
Max speed:　321 kt (369 mph) at 5,600 m (18,375 ft)
Climb rate:　7 min 22 sec to 6,000 m (19,685 ft)

1 m
1 2 3 ft

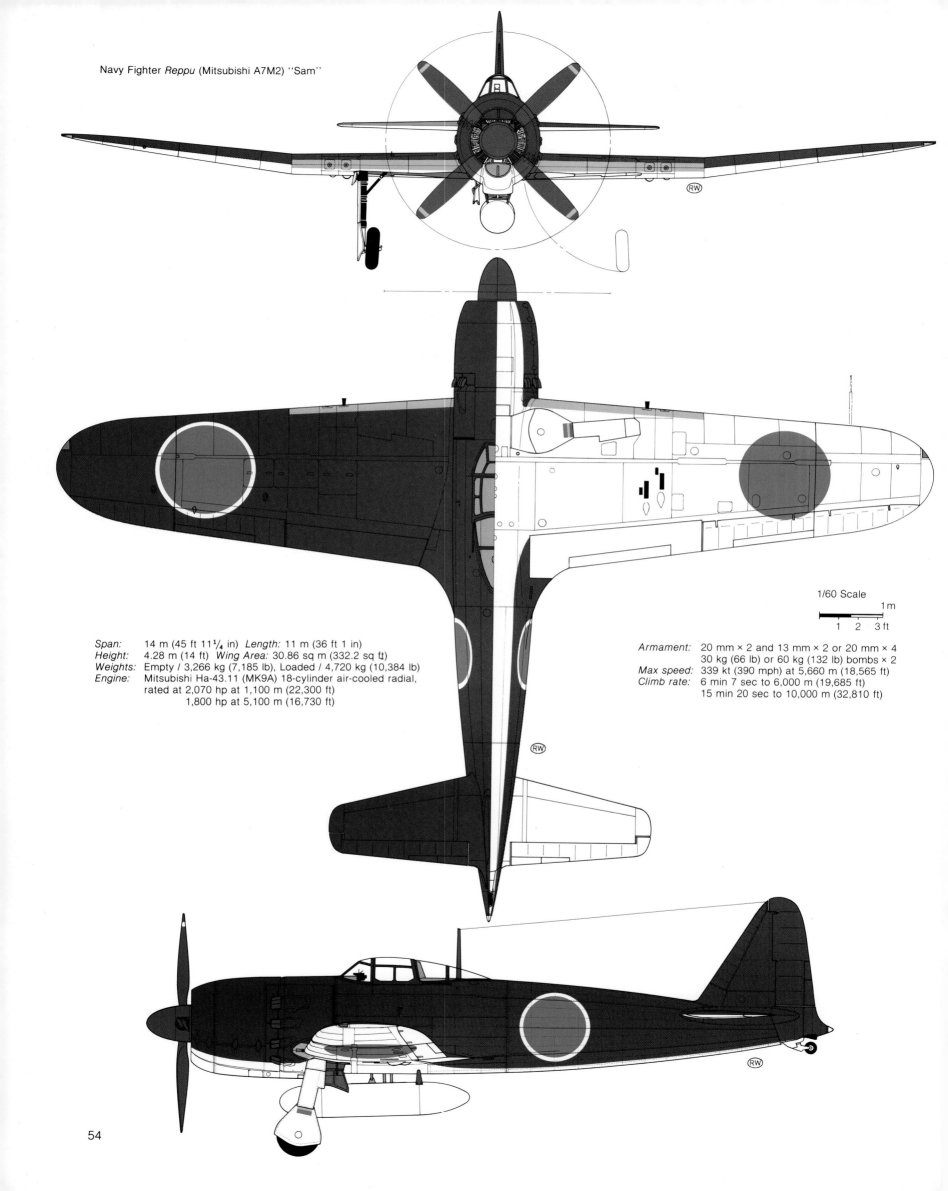

Navy Fighter *Reppu* (Mitsubishi A7M2) "Sam"

Span: 14 m (45 ft 11¼ in) *Length:* 11 m (36 ft 1 in)
Height: 4.28 m (14 ft) *Wing Area:* 30.86 sq m (332.2 sq ft)
Weights: Empty / 3,266 kg (7,185 lb), Loaded / 4,720 kg (10,384 lb)
Engine: Mitsubishi Ha-43.11 (MK9A) 18-cylinder air-cooled radial,
　　　　rated at 2,070 hp at 1,100 m (22,300 ft)
　　　　1,800 hp at 5,100 m (16,730 ft)

1/60 Scale

Armament: 20 mm × 2 and 13 mm × 2 or 20 mm × 4
　　　　30 kg (66 lb) or 60 kg (132 lb) bombs × 2
Max speed: 339 kt (390 mph) at 5,660 m (18,565 ft)
Climb rate: 6 min 7 sec to 6,000 m (19,685 ft)
　　　　15 min 20 sec to 10,000 m (32,810 ft)

A single Zero in a *kamikaze* attack the instant before it crashed into the battleship *USS Missouri* off Okinawa.

Due to many underlying factors, the ultimate production goal of the "Sam" was never achieved. The indecisiveness between Mitsubishi and the Navy over the selection of the engine to be used was the first of many delays. Once the decision was made, which was contrary to designer Horikoshi's choice, the necessary redesign caused additional delays, later to be compounded by material shortages, Allied bombing and the devastating earthquake in December, 1944.

When the prototype first flew 6 May, 1944, it possessed excellent stability and controllability, but was decidedly underpowered. At the Navy insistence, a less-powerful engine was used than Mitsubishi had planned. The *Homare* 22 engine, rated at 1,999 hp at take-off fell off with altitude until at 6000 m (19,700 ft) the engine was yielding only 1,300 hp. Intending to eliminate this shortcoming, a later prototype flew with the 2,200 hp Mitsubishi Ha 43 engine, and it was immediately obvious that manoevrability, rate of climb, and maximum speed were noticably improved, while it retained its excellent stability and control features.

When the war ended, only eight prototype A7M "Sam" fighters, with a few additional production models in the assembly stage, had been achieved. Thus, the true intended replacement fighter for the Zero had not flown one operational strike against the enemy, which by then was destroying the very factories from which these fighters were to come.

Kamikaze

From the early days over China and the first year of the Pacific war, the Zero was a living legend. Countless hordes of these nimble fighters would appear, seemingly from out of nowhere, attacking and sending their enemies to the ground in flames, then flamboyantly departing the battle area with barrel rolls pronouncing victory. The success of the Zero fighter in the early stages of the war can scarcely be over-emphasized. It was justifiably respected as the aggressor and victor.

As the final stages of the war turned to successive defeats for the Japanese, the Zero remained essentially the same aircraft that had fought four years earlier. With increased demands placed upon it, improvements were frequently made in attempts to at least match its opponents. Its engine was more reliable and somewhat more powerful. Design changes had improved its performance in some areas, and downgraded it in others due to added weight. An increase in weaponry gave it a bigger punch in striking power.

None the less, as the newer generation of Allied aircraft came on the scene, it became a losing battle whichever way the Zero turned to disengage from its enemy. The Japanese pilots were still just as courageous as in the early years of the Zero. For the young Japanese pilots who first flew the Zero, it was the modern weapon of the *samurai*, a nimble fighter not unlike the slashing sword with which Japan would defeat all its enemies. Now the situation in combat was reversed and the Zero had become the *hara-kiri* blade, an instrument of sacrificial suicide, a one-way expendable weapon that carried its pilot to death and glory. Consequently, the Zero itself, once victorious in combat was being expended in a cause that would elude its certain defeat.

The story of *kamikaze* attacks is not new. Few may realize, however, that more Zeros were expended in those attacks than any other aircraft, including special craft designed for these suicide missions. Normally the older Zeros, such as A6M2s, were fitted with a 250 kg (550 lb) bomb for these one-way missions. Initially volunteer crews were limited to those having less flying experience and who stood little chance of survival in air-to-air combat or accurate dive-bombing, but who would be able to guide their aircraft in a final death dive upon an Allied ship. The few experienced pilots that remained often flew escort in the later model Zeros that had a better chance of survival while acting as decoys to draw the fire of the aggressive F6F Hellcat fighter screens, and the walls of anti-aircraft which the U.S. fleet was able to set up.

The Battle of the Philippines, in October, 1944, was the first major operation to employ these tactics. Several American aircraft carriers were either sunk or severely damaged, along with other surface craft. Although these attacks were effective, they failed to prevent the U.S. forces from landing on Luzon, completing their invasion operations when and where they chose. Of the 331 Zeros launched in the Philippine Operation in *kamikaze* attacks, 158 were able to reach their targets, destroying themselves in this desperate manner of attack.

These tactics were used again during the invasion of Okinawa and other lesser locations throughout the ever tightening ring of combat around Japan. Had it not been for the surrender that took place before the pending invasion of Japan became necessary, the plan called for every Zero and comparable aircraft to be expended against the invading force in *kamikaze* attacks.

The philosophy of the *kamikaze* pilots had never been properly understood by Western minds, although many Western pilots died in missions which were virtually suicidal. Anyone having flown numerous combat missions has at one time or other felt that "his number" was up on a particular mission, yet continued on after there was still time to turn back to safety. A vivid example is the story of U.S. Navy Torpedo Squadron Eight at Midway as each plane attacked and was successively shot down. Not only have airmen demonstrated this bravery, but other combatants as well. One of many examples was the case of 20-mm gun crews remaining at their stations aboard the USS *Essex* until enveloped in flames, in an effort to beat off a *kamikaze* attack.

There was a fundamental difference however in the heroism of these opposing military men. The Japanese accepted the situation that there was no avenue of hope and escape – the American never did. To the Western mind there must be that last slim chance of survival, the feeling that

(National Archives)

although a lot of other men around him may die, it was he that somehow was going to make it back.

The Japanese pilots who accepted the principle of suicide tactics most wholeheartedly were, as a general rule, those whose religious or patriotic conviction were highly developed. These self-sacrificing attacks offered them a chance to attain several goals. Uppermost was to inflict losses on the enemy that might make them lose their overwhelming material advantage, while another motivation was to die bravely in the purest style of ancient Japanese tradition. Those who succeeded in returning from the typical type of combat encounters in which most of their comrades had been shot down were convinced that their survival was only temporary. A *kamikaze* mission afforded the opportunity to control this destiny in the form of a devastating blow against the enemy for love of family and country.

These examples of human self-sacrifice on a group scale have not been witnessed since the Pacific conflict. Perhaps a combat situation since then has not fostered such extreme measures. However, it seems doubtful, based on the attitudes so often expressed today, that a trend of such emotional human involvement would not be given a fleeting chance for consideration.

And yet the attraction of the hero remains in all the world; people still like to read about bravery and self sacrifice, even if it seems that there are fewer around who would appreciate it. Perhaps it is a cyclical thing; heroism may once again come into fashion, and the bravery of the men who flew the Zeros will become not only admirable, but understandable.

零式艦上戦闘機取扱説明書　海軍航空本部

緒言　本書ハ零式艦上戦闘機ノ取扱ニ関スル基準ヲ概説シタルモノニシテ取扱者ノ参考ニ資スルヲ以テ目的トス　本書記載ノ諸元ハ計画上乃至ハ実験機ニ依リ得タル数値ナルガ各機体ハ若干ノ許容差ヲ有スルガ故ニ各機附属ノ来歴簿記載事項ニ通暁シ其ノ完成検査成績表ニ依リ固有ノ諸元ヲ確メ飛行成績表ニ依リ之ガ性癖ヲ熟知スルヲ要ス　オ